THE
FOOD AND PEOPLE
DILEMMA

A New Collection By Duxbury Press.

THE MAN — ENVIRONMENT SYSTEM IN THE LATE TWENTIETH CENTURY

General Editor
WILLIAM L. THOMAS
California State University, Hayward

The Food and People Dilemma	*Georg Borgstrom*
Human Geography in a Shrinking World	*Ronald Abler, Donald Janelle, Allen Philbrick and John Sommer*
Urban Circulation Noose	*James D. Wheeler*

THE
FOOD AND PEOPLE
DILEMMA

GEORG BORGSTROM

Georg Borgstrom

Margaret and Tom with best wishes

for 1974 from Greta + Georg.

DUXBURY PRESS

North Scituate, Massachusetts
A Division of Wadsworth Publishing Company, Inc.
Belmont, California

Duxbury Press
A Division of Wadsworth Publishing Company, Inc.

ISBN-087872-050-2

L. C. Cat. Card No. 73-80016

Printed in the United States of America

1 2 3 4 5 6 7 8 9 10 - - 76 75 74 73

This book is dedicated to
my wife Greta
my invaluable helper

Contents

Editor's Foreword

In the year 1974, which has been designated by the United Nations as the "World Population Year," this important work is most timely. The United States is experiencing an era of heightened awareness of multiple crises, including rising inflation, energy shortages, and curtailed food production by those manufacturers caught between holding the line on retail prices and having to meet increased expenses for agricultural raw materials. It is too simple to suggest only that more and more food must be produced and distributed to feed ever more people. Placing the world's population explosion into historical perspective, this work points out that the numbers of the undernourished and undereducated are increasing dramatically because they are surviving infancy and living longer. And the largest increases in population are occurring in precisely those areas of the world where hunger is most common, so that by 1985 nearly three-quarters of the world's peoples will live in food-deficit regions.

A thorough examination is given to the relations of food production to the other elements in the man-environment system. For example, a nation's food supply supports man's domesticated animals as well as humans; world trade removes little of the inequities of regional food production and often is achieved only through soil degradation or by lowering the nutritive well-being of the citizens of exporting countries. As a result of urbanization, sixty percent of the world's people will live in cities by the end of the 20th century, mostly as a result of rural expulsion before urban employment and facilities are ready for the deluge. The "urban trap" heightens the aggravation of pollution and wastes created by human sewage, by the concentration of food processing plants, and by the animal "factories" to feed city populations. Exploiting minerals for fertilizers, mounting water use, and dumping into the ocean all have been gross factors in man's impact upon nature. Food production, likewise, has become increasingly dependent upon a massive use of energy. There is energy used in making farm equipment, in producing fertilizers and insecticides, in moving the farm machinery, in processing and packaging food products, and in all of the transportation and marketing that conveys agricultural products from farm to consumer. The author calls for a full and honest accounting of our energy budget. The Hunger Gap among nations is exceeded by an Energy Gap.

Here is a volume which explores the interactions of agriculture with food processing, transportation, industry, urbanization, and energy consumption. Its author, Georg Borgstrom, is exceptionally well qualified to present such an integrated view. He is Professor of Geography and of Food Science and Human Nutrition at Michigan State University, where he has been since 1956. Before then, Dr. Borgstrom was a professor and head of two major food research institutes in his native Sweden. He is a recognized authority on world food resources and their utilization and food freezing, with special interest in fish and fruits. His geographical studies explore the balance between population growth, world trade, and the contribution of fisheries to world food supplies, especially the use of protein. His major publications are: *Fish as Food* (editor of four volumes, 1960-64), *Japan's World Success in Fishing* (1964), *The Hungry Planet* (1965), *Principles of Food Science* (2 volumes, 1965), *Too Many, A Study of the Earth's Biological Limitations* (1969), *World Food Resources* (1973), and *Focal Points* (1973). Dr. Borgstrom has lectured widely on all continents except Australia (and Antarctica). He is a Fellow of the World Academy of Arts and Sciences, and recipient in 1969 of his university's Distinguished Faculty Award. The world has, indeed, been his classroom.

This work is one of a series of volumes to be published in the series, "The Man-Environment System in the Late 20th Century." The series as a whole brings to the literate public the fruits of geographic research deserving of a wider audience. A renewal of geography has taken place during the last several decades. The works in this series are reflective of a dynamic cross-disciplinary problem-solving attitude, with emphasis upon the geographer's role in man's management of his environment. Each volume in the series is intended as an integrated set of seven to nine essays on a topic close to its author's heart. Their collective purpose is to widen your intellectual horizon through familiarity with a geographic viewpoint.

WILLIAM L. THOMAS

Preface

This brief study is aimed not only at elucidating the complexity of the food-and-people issue, but also at bringing into clear focus its historical and biological dimensions. Questionable tacit assumptions and fallacies have been accepted and allowed to blur our vision far too long. Both in public debate and expert analysis the balance between food and people has been narrowed to a seemingly simple matter of more food and less people. Thinking has been dangerously eclipsed. Two major flaws in particular have dominated not only thinking but, what is worse, action programs. On one hand, scant recognition has been given to the dynamics of the intimate interplay between food and people. On the other, attention has not been paid to the complex ramifications of this issue, comprising a whole network of factors equally as vital as food and people.

We must also put an end to the prevalent habit of narrowing the field of perception, either by putting on blinders or resorting to verbal tranquilizers. The food-and-people issue is of such a paramount significance to man's future that we not only must boldly remedy our handling of these matters but also, and perhaps more importantly, submit our thinking to drastic revisions. This study constitutes an effort to open up new vistas by moving the debate out of dead center into constructive, progressive action.

All data compiled in this book originate with official government publications or with the United Nations agencies. Figures which have been computed by the author (indicated by an "A" over the column) are also based on such data. Only tables that are essential to the comprehension of the discussion are inserted in the text. The reader who so desires may refer to the statistical documentation contained in the Supplementary Tables, as frequently they contribute to a broader grasp of the issues analyzed. In particular, they should be useful to college students and experts. In the running text, references to all tables are held to a minimum to avoid distracting the reader.

Throughout the text and in many of the tables reference is made to the Hungry World (HW) and the Satisfied World (SW). The HW comprises those countries whose average per capita intake of food stays below minimum requirements, primarily Asia (exclusive of Japan), Latin America (exclusive of Argentina and Uruguay), and Africa. The SW comprises those countries whose average per capita intake of food is above minimum requirements (sometimes subdivided into the Well-fed and the Intermediary Group), primarily North America, Europe, the U.S.S.R., Australia, New Zealand, Japan, Argentina and Uruguay.

Georg Borgstrom

East Lansing, Michigan,
February, 1973.

Illustrations

Supplementary Tables

Chapter 1

The Golden Age

Although man appeared on earth more than one million years ago, only in the post-glacial period did he emerge as a dominant species with world-wide distribution. At first his numbers increased at exceedingly slow rates. Human population amounted to only a quarter-billion (by recent estimates) at the beginning of the Christian era. It took sixteen centuries to double this number, the first billion being reached as late as 1820. The second billion was reached only 110 years later (1930). Then came the awesome acceleration; in 1960, only 30 years later, the third billion had been added. Unbelievably, mankind is now in the unprecedented situation of adding almost another billion during the single decade of the seventies (App. Tables 1 and 2).

The present global population upsurge had its counterpart in the European population explosion, which peaked about the opening of the 20th century but had its major spectacular growth in the 100-year period, 1850 to 1950. Experts frequently cite medical advances as the major stimulus for this upsurge in population, and most textbooks emphasize the following sanitary improvements: (1) the creation of waterworks coupled with sewage disposal facilities, (2) the introduction of mass vaccination, and (3) the compulsory measures taken for the pasteurization of milk. Unquestionably each of these innovations drastically reduced mortality, particularly among infants, and as the number of individuals surviving to adulthood increased, the potential number of humans likewise increased. Basically, however, medical advances and improved sanitation do not adequately explain this tremendous population growth, nor its explosive nature. Other forces, set in motion when Europeans swarmed over all corners of the globe and tapped into a world-wide support system, are far more significant.

Europeanization of the World

The enormous demographic expansion which played a large part in the global spread of Western culture, has sometimes been called the *Europeanization of the world.* This led to the military and economic dominance of Europe over other continents. White supremacy, thus placed in its historical and demographic context, depends not on superior mental or physical endowments, but on rapid population increase, in turn built on reckless and diligent purveying with the full implementation of technology — yet basically resting upon the grabbing and ear-marking of vast land and soil resources outside the Western main as circumscribed by history.

The European Population
Explosion, 1850-1950

Europeans multiplied sixfold in three centuries, while the total of all other peoples was augmented only threefold. After representing only about 20 per cent of the world's population in 1650, Europeans had increased to almost 40 per cent by the year 1950, including descendents in other lands (App. Table 3). The big splash occurred between 1850 and 1950, adding around 580 million more. The losses of two world wars did little to change the picture. In the century of European glory, Europe multiplied 2.8 times, while Asia multiplied 1.3 and Africa 1.6 times. Although the declining European growth rate since 1950 forebodes a lessening share of world population in future generations, the estimates of population by continents portray a steady and decisive increase in the population of European descent. The 1950 total of 935 million people is almost exactly eight times the number three centuries earlier. Compare this rate to twice for Africa and less than four times for Asia (App. Table 1).

The Great Migration
(The Big Grab)

During the Golden Age (1850-1950), Europeans swarmed all over the globe. In the North American prairie they created a colony in tilled acreage, forest lands, and in mineral wealth far richer than the combined resources of all the European countries from which they came. In addition, the South American pampas were earmarked for their use. White man, in the guise of these European emigrants, also grabbed major choice pieces of the highland soils of Africa and took power positions of trade along the African coast. During this process India became British; the East-Indies became Dutch. Furthermore, the entire continent of Australia and its invaluable satellite New Zealand had become part of the white man's booty. This world-wide grab induced the greatest migration in history. Nearly 100 million left the European continent, although about one-fourth eventually returned, for a net exodus of 75 million. These millions became the progenitors of hundreds of millions more of European descent around the globe, primarily in North America, Latin America, Oceania, and Siberia.

The European Splurge, 1850-1950 (in millions)

	Europe	North America	Latin America	Oceania	(Russia) U.S.S.R.	Asia	Africa
1850	202	26	33	2	64	749	95
1950	392	166	163	13	180	1,384	222
Increase*	190	140	130	11	116	635	127**
Per Cent	94	537	394	550	181	85	134

* Secondary effects of the European population explosion (up to vertical line).
** Some European influx.

The European swarming was the greatest migration in human history, superseding the previous Chinese transfer to the other side of the infamous wall which separated pastoral lands from the plowed expanses of China. The European migration is the first one which can be classified as truly global, both in regard to geographical dimensions and in its repercussions. The current population explosion is forcing a still greater exodus of peoples: the huge influx into cities during the 1970's involves more than 600 million. This migration will be discussed in Chapter 7.

In 1907 the European migration peaked in the United States at a level of 1.2 million and remained close to that annual figure until 1913. This enormous influx of people created some of the most populous German, Polish, and Italian cities in the world. Interestingly enough, more people of Scandinavian ancestry now live in North America than in the Nordic countries.

The European imprint and impact affected the entire Western hemisphere. The Spanish and Portuguese broke into the Aztec and Inca empires in the 16th century and became the spearhead of the European push into the "new lands," bridging north and south.

In the second half of the 19th century, Western man seriously renewed his conquest of the vast powerhouse of Siberia with its riches of forests, soils, minerals, and fuel, a land once visualized as the New America (Borgstrom, *The Hungry Planet*, 1972, p. 231). The adversities and vagaries of the climate, however, have always set vigorous limitations on complete exploitation of Siberia (at least in its northern half) without huge food deliveries from the outside.

The Slave Trade. During his odyssey into the Western hemisphere, such enormous potentialities fell into the lap of the white man that at the time he could not take care of them, far less exploit them. So in the initial phases, prior to the great exploitation and fill-up after 1850, manpower was acquired from Africa through the infamous slave trade. Western man wrote some of the most disgraceful chapters of his entire social history by joining and expanding the hunting raids around Africa that had been initiated by the Arabs more than a millennium before. It has been estimated that some 40 to 50 million Africans were involved in this operation, with 15 million Africans being brought to the Americas. The wastage in human lives in the dispatching ports, on board the slave ships, in the receiving harbors and prior to the final settling was formidable.

Three points related to the food-and-people issue should be emphasized here. First, the influx of African labor dwindled in relative significance after the mid-19th century when the great European tidal wave started rising. Second, of the 15 million slaves brought to the Western hemisphere, only about one-half million reached the United States. Thus, in historical and biological perspective, one-half million Africans was minor in comparison to the 35 million European immigrants to the United States. This discrepancy is reflected even today in the lesser proportion of blacks (now increased to 12 per cent of the total population), many of whom carry European "blood." The third aspect of importance to the food-and-people issue is that African slave labor not only became instrumental but also indispensable to the development of the Western sugar empire in the Caribbean, led by Great Britain and France. This creation became a benefactor of Western man, but unquestionably a malefactor to the victimized slaves. The entire West Indies was organized to provide cheap and ample calories to the industrializing millions of Europe. The effect undoubtedly had an influence in pushing the European population figures upward and also in disassociating thinking, politics, and economy from awareness of the prime role of land and agriculture in the feeding of man and livestock. This sugar festival was the first "trip" in the European swindle of inebriation. The second, almost simultaneous, intoxicating drink was the great expansion of ocean fishing, in particular the long-distance hauling of codfish from the Grand Banks to provide inestimable high-rate protein.

Latin American Vignettes. The Conquest (la Conquista) of Latin America clearly resulted from the "pull" of the alleged treasures of the new lands. No critical "push" factor appears to have been involved. Both Spaniards and Portuguese were at the start attracted by the populated islands. They were, however, soon faced with labor shortages, which resulted in the endorsing and encouraging of the slave trade, spearheaded by the Portuguese already occupying the Atlantic stepping stones, the Azores, Madeiros, and the Cape Verde Islands.

It was only during the last hundred years that South America received its big European influx — Italians, Spaniards, Portuguese, Germans, Poles, Scandinavians, and others. The Portuguese dominated in Brazil, the

Spaniards in Mexico, and the Spaniards and Italians together in Argentina, where incidently, the business world was firmly controlled by the British.

More than half of the population of Argentina and one-fourth of all Brazilians claim to be of Italian descent. Germans became a surprisingly prevalent element in the São Paulo region and the two southern states of Brazil, as well as in the temperate part of Chile. They also took over large tracts of Central America as coffee growers. Scandinavians formed a colony in Misiones in northern Argentina.

The European era has been identified as the modern period of Latin America. The new ethnic element superimposed itself upon the Indian communities or formed delineated colonial enclaves. This European influence continues to create tensions over major parts of Latin America, mainly because of the economic allegiance to their homelands.

U.S. Immigration.   Immigration to the United States falls into three fairly well-defined phases. Until 1890 most immigrants came from countries in northern and western Europe, mainly the British Isles, Germany, the Scandinavian countries, the Netherlands, and Switzerland, although during this period, Chinese laborers were imported to provide manpower for railroad building, canneries, and laundries (App. Table 5).

The second phase, from 1890 to about 1930, saw the majority of immigrants come from the countries of southern and eastern Europe, notably Italy, former Austria-Hungary, and Russia. While the overwhelming majority of immigrants have always come from Europe, after 1910 this dominance was slightly affected by a secondary influx from Canada and Mexico, although largely composed of people of European origin. This shift became increasingly marked after 1921 and was affected by laws which restricted movements from Europe.

Origin of U.S. Immigration, 1820-1930   (in millions)

Europe	32.27
No. & W. Europe	(18.33)
So. & E. Europe	(13.94)
Canada	2.90
Mexico	0.76
West Indies	0.43
Other countries	0.90
Total	37.26

A third phase was initiated after World War II, when many of the uprooted, often relatives of earlier immigrants, sought a haven in the United States. New rules established in the 1960's, which removed special quotas, created an upsurge in the number of immigrants from Latin America and Asia (the Philippines, Korea, Taiwan and India). Even so, it is worth noting that the European flow still dominates (App. Table 4).

The Canadian Replica. At the time of Confederation (1867) most Anglo-Canadians were children and grandchildren of settlers who had come from the United States. Few immigrants came directly from England until the prairies opened up in the latter part of the 1870's. The second founding element was the French, who with impressive tenacity performed a unique feat of human reproductiveness. From a few thousand who arrived in the 17th century, with only minor additions until the year 1760, Canada counted in the 1960's more than 5.5 million French, excluding a million who migrated to New England during the 19th century. Hundredfolding in two centuries is truly record-breaking. As a result the Eastern part of Canada was less significant as an outlet for Europe's overflow. This development also portrays the irony of history, since France was one of the few European countries that took the teachings of Malthus to heart — slow population growth resulting in less population pressure — while Malthus' homeland, England, followed the optimistic French school of the Utopians and Progressivists, exhibiting rapid growth and critical population pressures. (See p. 13 and p. 25 for further discussion of the Malthusian doctrine.)

Since Confederation almost 10 million immigrants have come to Canada (App. Table 6). This influx had *made* Canada and still is a decisive factor. Approximately one in seven Canadians is a postwar immigrant. During peak years in that period, around a quarter-million were admitted: 282,-164 in 1957, and 222,876 in 1967.

Nevertheless, the founding peoples of Canada (the French and British) still represent approximately 74 per cent of the present population. Indians and Eskimos account for a little above one per cent. The remaining quarter show the traditional array of peoples, with Germans constituting the largest group. Italians started to arrive in a trickle in the 1880's, but have been the major group since 1950. They are on the verge of overtaking the Ukrainians as the fourth-largest ethnic group in Canada. The European splurge in the Canadian setting is very much a replica of what happened on the United States scene. Although there always has been a movement back and forth between the United States and Canada, a new element in the 1960's was an increase in immigrants from the United States as well as from the Caribbean.

Immigrants to Canada (in thousands):
Annual average 1965-67
(by country of birth)

Britain	50.7	Germany	7.5
Italy	31.1	Caribbean	6.2
U.S.	14.1	France	5.4
Portugal	8.6	Others	56.3
Greece	8.2	Total	188.1

The Postwar Aftermath. It is worth noting that the United States and Canada still constitute a significant outlet for the excess millions of Europeans (App. Tables 4 and 6). Despite some quota adjustments which raised the relative number of migrants from Asia and Latin America, the lion's share still comes from Europe. Remember, too, that Latin Americans are primarily late-generation descendants of European stock. Although the numbers migrating into North America are less than in the peak years of the big wave, the pattern remains basically the same. North America asserts itself as the great haven of Western man, despite the many hundred millions more who have been added during the postwar period to the vast non-European world.

How About Asia? Political commentators express concern that the Asian populations will overwhelm all others. They stress that Asians already constitute more than one-half of the world's peoples and will swell to two-thirds prior to the year 2000. Such reasoning, however, fails to consider both the historical and biological dimensions of these trends. The peoples of Asia, Africa, and Latin America were cultural predecessors of Europeans, producing all major civilizations and religions. The notion that they are following us in making the alleged demographic transition to a balanced population overlooks the fact that they have become critically overdeveloped through the millennia, and particularly during the last century. They have mobilized their land, soil, forests, and water to the limit, generating critical imbalances between population and resources.

The Last Trail

There has been constant debate in sociological and economic studies of the relative significance of the forces exercising the greatest influence on the great European trek, whether it was the "pull" — the prospects for a better life — or the "push," as manifested in the growing land shortage of Europe and in imbalances there between industrialization and the degree and rate of employment. The push and the pull coincided, however, in the food and resource issue. Never in history did a group of men procure a greater bounty than those who came to the northern flank of the western hemisphere with its great resources in land, soils, forests, and minerals. The North American prairie has no counterpart in any other continent. The real exploitation of these riches was telescoped in time to not much more than one hundred years.

Americans tend to picture their accomplishments as a big sweep, spanning a whole continent, when the Anglo-French thrust from the North and Northwest finally joined hands with the Spanish from the South and Southeast and the Russian from the Northwest. Spain and Russia had both overexpanded, and California, Alaska, and later Hawaii, became swept up into the great Western thrust. The lesson to be drawn from this historical maneuver is that Western man opened up his last frontier, and in so doing, blazed his last trail.

The billions of people in the non-Western world cannot match this drive — there are no new continents to exploit. The populations of India, China, and the Middle East have no new America to turn to for food. Where would China or India find new lands, as Europe did in the prairie, from which to feed their forthwelling millions to the combined tune of almost 30 million people per year? The world could not possibly meet an overseas demand corresponding to that of present-day Europe. There is even less likelihood of these hungry nations following the Japanese model, still more excessively fed from extraterritorial sources.

China and India — Net Import of Cereals:
predicated on the Overseas Models of Europe
and Japan (million metric tons)

1967-69	Net Import	Kilograms per capita	On European model	On Japanese model
Europe	25.5	56.3	—	156.4
Japan	12.5	124.0	56.3	—
China & India	10.6	7.9	75.0	168.0

The conclusion, however, is the same for both sides of the Gap. The Western world has to apply the brakes on human growth in order to reduce its grand scale exploitation of the globe. It is also going to be forced to gain control of its growing numbers in order to avert further nutritional impairment or, even worse, to avoid mounting mortalities. Any gains that are made need to accrue to those now living and to the betterment of their lot.

The Golden Age of Western Man

The European branch of the human family not only staged the greatest migration in history but further improved its situation by (1) developing transoceanic and transcontinental transportation, (2) applying canning and refrigeration to food preservation, and finally (3) procuring higher yields through a massive input of science and technology.

Equally significant was the fact that these advances almost exclusively were mobilized, not to feed all of the world's people, but to provide for a select group of Europeans who felt the pressure of people and the need for expanded resources. Only vaguely was the dualism of this pressure recognized, namely the intertwining or even reversal of cause and effect. This whole upheaval may be described in technical terms as an explosion, but equally well and perhaps more adequately as biological gross dynamics, as a growth in numbers resulting from satisfactory feeding.

The Transportation Upheaval

The European reshaping of global transportation had a particularly dramatic effect upon the food scene. The emergence of the combustion engine and the discovery of easily handled liquid fuel (petroleum) introduced an entirely new concept — for the first time cities of a million people could be fed. Studies about early Asian cities, allegedly of that size, and previous statements to that effect about the city of Rome have not stood the test of renewed historical scrutiny. Their inhabitants numbered about 350,-000 and never exceeded a half-million. The haulage of grains, rice from the Indonesian archipelago to the Asian mainland, and wheat and barley across the Mediterranean from the Nile Valley, Carthage, and later from Scythia (Ukraine), was limited in volume because of the small size of the vessels and the slow movement by oars and sails. Through clipper ships Europe and North America created a grand finale to this stage, and at the same time introduced the initial phase of what later became a large-scale global transfer of grain from Australia and the South American pampas to rapidly over-filling Europe.

The transportation revolution also contributed indirectly to the global creation of Western feeding bastions. Key features of this mercantilistic drive were the build-up of the Caribbean sugar empire, of the meat industry of Argentina and Uruguay, the butter and mutton potency of New Zealand, and not least, the plantation enterprises for cotton, oilseeds, bananas, cacao, and coffee.

The Golden Age saw the capacity of the vessels swell and the velocity rise. For the first time in history hunger vanished from the North American prairies and from the farmlands of Europe. As late as 1850 to 1870, years of hunger and starvation are documented in Scandinavia, Germany and France. The minor classic, *Giants in the Earth* by O. E. Rolvaag (1927), about Norwegian pioneers in North Dakota in the latter part of the 19th century, vividly describes the equally harsh limitations of the prairies whenever drought, locusts, or frost hit. This is a salutary reminder of the shortages even the affluent West someday may face. It also illustrates the degree to which Western man commissioned the entire globe for his well-being with little concern until the 1950's for the legitimate needs of the other three-fourths of the world's people.

As in Europe, North American cities of a million or more exist only on the basis of long-distance hauling. Transcontinental railways and a vast network of highways spanning the North American and Eurasian continent constitute indispensable prerequisites for the feeding of these huge conglomerates, not to mention the enormous inputs of energy required for the haulage of at least one million pounds of food each day for every million inhabitants. Education has failed to convey to most Westerners, and in particular to each American, an awareness of this dependence on distant prairie soils, dairy farms, feed lots, and rangelands. This large-scale feeding from many thousands of miles away contributed drastically to the Western world's losing touch with ecological realities. In fact, it is a key factor of the present crisis. Technology has not changed in one iota man's basic dependence on soil, water, and food.

Food Technology

Another important feature of this ominous hundred-year Golden Age was the technical advances in food processing, marked in particular by the development of canning and the mechanical refrigeration of food. Both processes required readily available fuel resources, a need which coincided with newly discovered coal and oil in Pennsylvania in 1856. As these fossil fuels were literally out of sight, they were soon taken for granted, becoming another invisible prerequisite for the daily life of Western man. Canning, for an entire century since its invention in 1810, had been used almost exclusively for military purposes. At the end of the century, however, it finally moved into broad civilian use through the creation of major food industries.

Mechanical refrigeration not only allowed the development of new freezing techniques, but also the transport of such perishables as eggs, meat and butter to Europe from distant sources, such as Australia, New Zealand and Argentina. Led by the United States, an almost super-human, incomprehensible surge of refrigerated vessels created a "Cold Tunnel" through the heat belt of the tropics. Thus invaluable supplementary food from the Southern hemisphere began to flow to the white man's depots.

Science Enters Agriculture

The turn of the century also saw the firm establishment of scientific agriculture, reflected in the development of seed control, use of commercial fertilizers and chemical sprays, and new breeds of crop plants and livestock. Furthermore, the scientific classification and preparation of soils vastly improved. Professorial chairs in agricultural chemistry were created in both Europe and czarist Russia. This trend was later manifested in the establishment of land-grant agricultural colleges in the United States.

It should be pointed out that science and agriculture did not mix overnight. Several European countries, under the pressure of their growing numbers, had been gradually introducing various practices geared toward higher returns from the fields. Some of these innovating measures date to the 17th and 18th centuries. Rotation schemes, root crops, and the growing of legumes are often mentioned as the methods that contributed most to greater productivity and to the feeding of more people. Less emphasized is the introduction of fencing, often at very great expense. Fencing was a prerequisite to both efficient animal production (farm-based and disassociated from pastures commonly owned or reached through transhumance) and to controlled breeding. In many countries like the United Kingdom fencing required greater investments than the construction of railways.

In historical retrospect, fencing stands out as perhaps the greatest single factor with long range impact on agriculture (as on the Spanish meseta, in the British Isles, and in Central Europe). Even when this empirical phase had run its course and science pioneered a more systematic and methodical approach, the gap between the needs of the millions and the "miracles of the land" was still widening. While the European ceiling was raised considerably, only in a few instances was it sufficient to accommodate all the added millions. At the time very few understood what was happening, and far less were aware that progress was also contributing toward an increased pressure of people which eventually gave way to the great Western trek.

More Food, More People

The European population explosion is largely explained by the massive migration to all corners of the globe, coupled with extraordinary measures taken to feed those who stayed home. The European section of the human family grew drastically in numbers, primarily by being provided with food through many new channels. This whole process may have been initiated and partly supported by the medical measures taken in the second half of the 19th century, but these would have been of no avail without the supplementary, successful efforts to feed the growing numbers of Europeans who now survived. Ample food also explains why Europeans grew more rapidly during the hundred-year period 1850 to 1950 than other branches of the human family. This trend switched around 1950. The world then returned to the old pattern, but with most of Latin America, Africa and Asia growing the fastest. Food, when increased in volume, has throughout history led to more people, and is presumably once again the determining factor in growth. As long as effective birth control measures are not taken, the prime effect is to multiply human misery.

Dispelling the Myths

History textbooks often blatantly reveal how poorly understood the European outflow is in biological and even historical terms. How Western man, almost for his exclusive survival, created huge beachheads around the world with little consideration for the world at large is disregarded. These vast supporting colonies were taken for granted as parts of the white man's domain, and the ensuing influx of food and feed is often considered evidence of the efficiency of the homeland agriculture rather than recognition of the enormous expansion in overseas real estate.

"The rationalization of husbandry resulted in an increase in output which ended once and for all the threat of famine. The last hunger in Europe came in the 1840's" — Yet millions of emigrants crossed the ocean to the Western hemisphere.

"The Agricultural Revolution insured an adequate food supply.

Only when war or revolution disrupted the international market was there a serious danger of food shortage. This change in attitude was a measure of how swiftly the food supply of Europe had grown during the previous one hundred and fifty years. The production of food ceased to be the occupation of the great majority of Europeans. Basic changes in the forms of human employment were made possible by expanding surpluses in agriculture. Without these surpluses there could have been no shift of population from country to city, from husbandry to manufacturing." -Yet, as discussed in Chapters 6 and 7, in several key countries the influx of food from transoceanic sources was an indispensable prerequisite for European urbanization in the wake of industrialization.

The monopolistic nature of these ventures is little heeded in historians' analyses: "The material welfare of mankind was increasingly based on a vast world market in which the interests of all nations converged and interacted." This statement mirrors in almost uncanny terms a gruesome and myopic ethnocentricity, or does it reflect callousness — that only Western man counts in history?

Some writers proudly point to the great improvements in ocean transportation, introduced during the 19th century, that made it possible for farmers overseas to feed and clothe the European consumer. "Wheat grown in the United States and Canada began to cross the Atlantic. Argentinian beef and Australian wool invaded the Continent. Subsistence farming everywhere retreated before commercial farming. Self-sufficiency became a mirage."* Nowhere in this fairy tale is there a recognition of the colossal broadening of the European feeding base that took place to parallel the great migration. The whole emphasis is on technique, almost completely overlooking the Big Grab.

It is not yet fully realized by the peoples of the industrialized nations of the West that their high standards of living have been—and, in part, are continuing to be—achieved by a massive exploitation of the world's total resources and a concomitant accumulation of capital. The first fruits of man's increasing control of nature fell to England, considered the birthplace of the Industrial Revolution, and was accompanied by a misery and degradation hardly paralleled at any time in history.

The Industrial Revolution of England served as the model of capitalism in the works of Karl Marx. To him, this transformation was a violent encroachment upon the lives of the English. All bounds of morals and nature were swept away by the insatiable demands of the burgeoning factory system and machine production. The peasants were torn from their rural holdings and forced or enticed into the slavery of the factories as pauperized laborers. Generations of women, children, and displaced farmers were blighted by the unplanned and unforseen consequences of this early revolution, brought about by science and technology.

*The quotations are from Lyon-Rowen-Hamerow (1970): *A History of the Western World.* Chicago (Rand McNally), p. 604-605.

What Marx never grasped, however, was that these inhuman conditions resulted from an unprecedented population upsurge. Major features he justly criticized were child and women labor, miserable housing conditions, extensive unemployment, and low salaries, but never in his thinking did he look behind the day-to-day scene and discover the push of growing numbers. From A.D. 1300 to 1700, the European population had remained almost stagnant. The feeding base did not considerably expand in terms of new lands or higher yields. Mortality was high, wars and diseases ravaged, and recurrent bad weather reduced crops to the point of causing food shortages. Certainly, hunger was no uncommon phenomenon in rural Europe. Only regional resources were available for supplementation.

England initiated the population parade by doubling its numbers from 1700 to 1800. During the 19th century the population quadrupled. The upsurge was almost as dramatic in other parts of Europe. The start of the real crisis came only in that century. After three to four decades, the "Hungry Forties" errupted, culminating in the revolutionary explosion of 1848, one year after Marx formulated and published his *Manifesto*. Frequently overlooked is the fact that this convulsion was preceded by famine years over most of Europe in the mid-1840's. Not until after this cataclysm did mortality start to decline decisively, setting in motion the critical upsurge in human numbers which led to the global outburst that for three centuries had been only a trickling outflow.

The Cardinal Issue: Food and People

Although industrialization boomed and world trade markets were opened, the numbers became overwhelming, such that employment could not remain abreast of the galloping population. Migration thus became the indispensable and inevitable outlet. The alternative, strongly advocated by Malthus, was population control in order to alleviate the immense suffering of the millions. He clearly saw the limitations of migration. In contrast to most comments about his *Essay*, he anticipated as well as analyzed the consequences of new technologies, but underlined that at best they would give only temporary relief. Without adjustments in population numbers, no permanent improvement could be reached. Because of its geometric growth (the compounded interest principle), population tended to overtake expansions in food production, as these inevitably were founded on the arithmetic principle. More food could be attained only by adding new lands, providing or tapping more water, or by employing more fertilizers. According to Malthus, both trade and irrigation were only large-scale deceptions, and historic development has proven him correct on all counts. His chief mistake lay in his firm conviction that population control was to be achieved only through abstinence and not through contraceptives — although they were on sale to the public at this time both in France and England.

The unquestionable fact remains that a population explosion—completely independent of economic systems—sharpens the struggle for survival. This has been the case throughout history. Marx failed to recognize these phenomena, and the present debate still remains under the same grave misapprehension. It is neither capitalism, as Marx believed, nor communism, as many Westerners maintain, that foster poverty and misery. It is the tragic imbalance between population and resources. In this regard the European situation around the turn of the century is in many ways a forerunner of the current world crisis, as it unfolds in unbelievable unemployment, critical scarcity of soils, minerals, and fuel, as well as in shortages of food and water. Only the Western minority is well-off, still reaping the benefits of its global grab.

There is another way of viewing this widening gap, its causes and nature; namely, that for one crucial century in the sequence of history, technology and economics created the unique opportunity to unfold their tricks without taking biology seriously into account. This might, in the long run, turn out to be mankind's greatest and most fateful mistake.

Chapter 2

The Global
Population Tide

The postwar upsurge in human numbers has been called an explosion, a phenomenon which is undoubtedly the most ominous feature of the human family. We have already witnessed one doubling in this very century, and a second doubling appears inevitable before the year 2000, barring any major catastrophe or large-scale famine. Such an increase in numbers is truly unprecedented in human history, yet most people, even many categories of experts, still seem to be unaware of the dimensions and true nature of this crisis.

Actually, the term "explosion," is not a very satisfactory description of present demographic trends. It is certainly not the question of a single dramatic happening. Rather, it is quite protracted in time and continually accelerating. Currently (1973) the world is growing by almost a billion per decade. Man added 76 million in 1972, but the annual figure will be 80 million in the late 1970's and 100 million in the 1980's. What is happening is better described as a tidal wave, constantly rising and inundating larger and larger areas. The world is witnessing an insidious, penetrating force of human numbers, persistently growing less and less manageable and accompanied by a disturbing deflation in most human values.

Despite courageous efforts by devoted groups, this crisis has not yet received the attention it desperately needs. Timid bureaucracies are caught in a striking discrepancy between thought and action. Although mankind is "hitting the ceiling" — reaching the limit in its use of the vital resources of soils, water and forests — it is obvious that nowhere in our population control measures have we moved beyond the limited tactics of family planning. True population control in the sense of a deliberate effort to bring down birth rates has been adopted in very few places. Limiting our efforts to averting "unwanted" children is wholly inadequate, as studies show that even if

successful, such a policy would have only marginal effects on world population growth by the year 2000. It seems highly unlikely that such a
growth rate can be sustained for very long without grave consequences to
man as well as to civilization. For this very reason speculation about the
year 2000 or still more distant times represents a dangerous escapism, poorly conducive to a realistic debate.

Why the Great Population Tide?

The present population surge is not the outcome of any fertility ram-
page. On the contrary, the fertility rate, defined as the number of babies
born per year to 1,000 women in potentially procreative age brackets, has
been declining almost everywhere. But the death rate has been descending
even more drastically, resulting in larger gains in net growth. This is the
least understood phenomenon. The rapid gains are predominantly due to
reduced infant mortality. Few realize that among the 2.5 billion who constitute the Hungry World (HW)*, more than half are below 18 years of age.
Yet more than half of all infants die before the age of five. The HW currently counts around one billion children, 650 million of whom will never reach
adulthood. To all these children life is nothing more than a Vigil of Death.

In the HW most statistical data about infant mortality, birth rates,
and the prevalence and frequency of diseases are shocking, yet they veil the
true adversities and inadvertently give an embellished accounting. In many
key regions of Latin America, Africa, and Asia, the births of children are
rarely ever registered until the age of three to five. Only when there are clear
indications that a child will survive infancy do parents and authorities submit to the red tape and cost of legal registration. It can therefore be safely
concluded that the dismal plight of children is much worse in reality than
demographic data indicate.

As infant mortality drops, however, more female youngsters reach
the child-bearing age. Because the age brackets in the developing world are
tilted toward the young, there are more prospective mothers per 1,000 of the
population. Thus, paradoxically, the birth rate (number born per year to 1,-
000 of the population) continues to climb despite a declining fertility rate.

Japan and many developing countries are currently showing such
soaring numbers. The United States is faced with a similar situation, in that
the baby boom after World War II has created a corresponding parent boom
in the late 1960's. In the 1970's, therefore, the United States will have 30 per
cent more women of child-bearing age. For this reason the fertility rate,
which has been dropping in the United States since 1957, must continue its

* The Hungry World (HW) comprises those countries where average per capita intake of
food stays below minimum requirements, primarily Asia (exclusive of Japan), Latin America
(exclusive of Argentina and Uruguay), and Africa.

present downward trend in order to avert a renewed spurt in population figures.

The acceleration of population growth, reflected in declining mortality figures, may also imply a longer life span related to improved living conditions. Sometimes these obvious considerations are disregarded because conventional statistics of per capita incomes and of actual levels of living do not include individual health, life expectations, or the possession of children.

Another consequence of these complex interrelationships is important when comparing countries on a per capita basis, on their intake of food and on their use of fuel, metals, or forests products. In comparing the United States with India, for instance, all per capita data reveal staggering discrepancies. Yet over time, the data for the United States need to be doubled to get the true figure of per capita consumption, since the average life span of each American is twice that of a person in India.

The Growing Food Spiral

Equally important to the food-and-people issue is the realization that even with zero population growth (ZPG) the amount of food needed will increase considerably, mainly because of the over-representation of young age-classes. When the 0-5 year olds reach the 10-15 year bracket, they will require a far greater daily intake per individual. For example, if ZPG became a reality in India today, 25-30 per cent more food would still be needed within a decade.

Another result, frequently overlooked, is that in the absence of adequate population control measures among the millions of malnourished, more food merely increases the numbers to feed. Unfortunately, less is then accomplished in truly alleviating hunger than in adding more numbers to the undernourished cadres through a higher survival rate (lowered mortality) and a lengthened life span.

The Losing Race

Returning to the overall global scene, the explosive growth in human numbers is threatening to wipe out the advances mankind has made and to undermine all human values, sinking a growing portion of mankind into abject poverty. Contrary to general belief and despite our countermeasures, the number of hungry, thirsty, poor, and illiterate is relentlessly increasing, both in relative and absolute terms. Their inadequacy has been veiled in embellishing rhetoric, and at best we have witnessed only temporary improvements.

Population Growth, by Continents in 1972

	Total population (in millions)	Annual net growth (per cent)	Average birth rate (per thous.)	Average death rate (per thous.)	Time for doubling (years)	Population under 15 yrs. of age (per cent)
Asia	2,154	2.3	37	14	30	40
Africa	364	2.6	47	21	27	44
Latin America	300	2.8	38	10	25	42
Europe	469	0.7	16	10	99	25
North America	231	1.1	17	9	63	29
U.S.S.R.	248	0.9	17.4	8.2	77	28
Oceania	20	2.0	25	10	35	32

This state of affairs has a number of far-reaching consequences. Even with strictly enforced birth control we cannot expect any spectacular reduction in human numbers in this century. Even so, drastic measures have to be taken within the 1970's if we are going to attain any meaningful redress toward a human balance. For example, in Asia, where the food deficit is the greatest, the population now exceeds 2 billion and is growing at 2.3 per cent annually (App. Table 7). In Asia alone there are 49 million more people to feed every year, and at the average rate of rice consumption, it takes over 10 million tons more rice every year to provide for these added numbers. Total United States rice production is 2.5 million tons — so world production must increase each year by four times that amount just to uphold the present level of rice consumption in Asia. Africa and Latin America are currently experiencing a still more rapid population expansion. No better example can be brought forth to illustrate the Malthusian principle and its working and to show how the food issue projects on the world scene.

It is food for thought that as a human family we have not succeeded in adequately taking care of the one billion added since the end of World War II, nor even the 2 billion added since 1900. Yet besides this formidable backlog we are facing an additional gigantic board-and-lodging task in the next ten years — when almost one billion more will be clambering onto our finite spaceship Earth. The losing race is also reflected in the growing numbers of illiterate adults, an additional 30 million per year on top of the already accumulated pile-up of 750 million.

Fallacious Thinking

Numerous fallacies and oversimplified sloganeering surround the crucial population issue — without a doubt the most important and gravest matter of our days. We are not the first generation faced with the urgent necessity of showing restraint. Although birth control was common practice in most advanced civilizations, ours seems to be the first to have fallen for the entirely false notion that the globe is limitless and that man's control of his destiny as well as of nature is supreme, the only limit being his resourcefulness. Several generations have been fostered under this serious misapprehension, resulting from a colossal failure of our education system. The fragmentation of our thinking, stewarded by specialization, has made us steer away from formulating goals and at the same time has made us forget our purposes. We have been caught in the disastrous fallacy of believing that by willing the means we will automatically attain the goals. We have reached mastery in tactical maneuverings but have been either poor strategists or woefully negligent ones.

Medical Advances

These blunders all receive their focus in the population issue. We blame the explosion on the medical profession, when it should be obvious to anyone that simple survival through medical devices does not explain the population growth. Instead it is the joint outcome of all measures taken to improve the food balance, not the least by producing more food and by transporting both food and water on a global scale, all without a strict control of human numbers.

That biological interrelationship is self-evident. Nevertheless, attention has been focused almost one-sidedly on the effect of medical advances on mortality figures, forgetting that a prerequisite to uphold the medical gains must be food for the added numbers.

Technological Innovation

Western man has made another tragic mistake in judgment by believing that high dependence on food vanished when his own sustenance base was moved out of sight to transoceanic or transcontinental lands. The idea that technological innovations freed man from his bondage to living nature and the creative forces of lands and seas has become so predominant that it has almost developed into a creed. Despite major advances such as irrigation, breeding, chemistry, disease control, and so on, which are to the credit of technology, man's basic dependence on the microbial world coupled with photosynthesis has not been affected. Many technological innovations merely serve to remedy man's destructive and depleting actions. Finally, technological innovations have not modified one iota man's requirements of air, food, water, and minerals, and if anything have only sharpened their relevance.

Contraceptive Techniques

We seriously seem to believe that thanks to the modern pharmaceutical industry we are the first generation groping for a firm control of births. Yet all advanced civilizations through history have practiced birth control in one form or other; admittedly some were practicing infanticide, but many other techniques and procedures prevailed. Modern features like the intra-uterine spiral and after-day-pills count their origin and discovery thousands of years ago. Coitus interruptus, despite other advances, is still the main birth control method in Italy as it was in ancient Rome; this practice is also quite prevalent in India. Unfortunately, despite the availability of contraceptives, abortions are taking the lives of an unnecessary number of mothers, a situation which preventive measures should supersede.

Far greater priority should be placed on the search for truly new and better methods of contraception and on ways toward universal acceptance of such practices. Our advances so far have resulted in devices which are too complicated and too costly. We have fallen victim to a peculiar obsession that contraceptive techniques need to be foolproof. Tremendous strides could be made with procedures and methods which are only ninety per cent effective.

Historical Dimensions of Population Growth

Our present dilemma cannot be properly understood until we explore the historical dimensions of these demographic phenomena. Early cultures depended upon hunting, fishing, and simple gathering of food. These activities could only support low population densities, varying from three inhabitants per 100 square miles in the more precarious conditions (Eskimos) to three per square mile in the most favorable conditions, as in the coastal areas where the standard means of subsistence could be supplemented with produce from the sea. In very early times climate was the main regulator of human evolution and its variations, which were quite considerable over a long period. Climate was also the causal origin of many important migrations.

The Agricultural Revolution

At the dawn of the agricultural revolution, some 8,000-10,000 years B.C., the population of the world probably numbered somewhere between 5 and 10 million. The organization of land resources for cultivation, following the domestication of favored plants for crops and certain animal species for livestock, led to the development of agriculture. This development was a factor in demographic expansion just as much as the urban revolution, which first appeared in the Nile Valley and in Mesopotamia about 4000 B.C., and one millenium later in the Indus Valley.

Current estimates of world population at the beginning of the Christian era oscillate about the figure of 250 million. Fifty-four million inhabitants are attributed to the Roman Empire at that time. Some 30 to 50 million lived around the Mediterranean, with only 6 to 7 million in the Roman homeland, present-day Italy. China then had about 70 million. Some 40 million has been considered a plausible figure for India in the 2nd century, B.C., and the figure remained relatively stable until year zero. Step by step original settlements were followed by migrations whose driving forces were chiefly man's interminable quest for more food and feed.

Migrations

All forms of migration basically had in common an insatiable demand for more land. Since all subsistence ultimately was derived from the land, more land usually meant better living conditions, a fact which prevailed whether subsistence ensued from hunting, cattle raising, agriculture, or industry. This urge for land induced man to spread step by step to all habitable corners of the globe. In doing so he came in contact with populations already occupying outlying regions; conflicts and race mixtures ensued. The contact of peoples also furthered cultural development by introducing divergent standards and practices, new ideas and methods, with the selection of the most expedient. Thus migration has been at the very base of the development of the human race and of human culture. The four most important types of migration recorded in history have generally been distinguished as invasion, conquest, colonization, and immigration.

Invasion is a large-scale movement of people into the territory of another group and is generally a concerted, hostile operation. Classic examples are the semi-barbaric tribes breaking into the countries of southern and western Europe, as in the invasions by the Goths, the Huns, the Vandals, and the Magyars. Other examples are the spread of the Arabs and Turks over northern Africa and into Europe.

Conquest, usually undertaken for glory and aggrandizement and not involving major transfers of population, is an invasion into a less-advanced region. Striking historical examples of such conquests are the making of an empire by Alexander the Great or the build-up of the Roman counterpart. The British takeover in India also had many of the characteristics of a conquest. It is the irony of history that the big colonial drive of the Western world, led by Spain, Portugal, the Netherlands, Britain and France, and later joined by Germany and Italy, offered very little outlet for the overflowing Western world. Rather the great haven (safety valve) for the outflow was to be in the temperate zones with the huge expanses of the prairies (when no longer in a colonial status) and the pampas. All Italian and German colonies in Africa prior to World War II held less immigrants from the homelands than the total population of Brooklyn.

This colonial drive was political and economic but still lingers on in the economic sphere, dictating the flow of goods, including agricultural products. There is a deeper biological reason, however, for this colonial drive. In much of the warm world Western man encountered two kinds of key areas — either those that were overfilled or those that were sparsely populated because Nature had raised insuperable obstacles to the feeding of any large numbers of immigrants. This basic fact is still reflected today in Latin America, where the more temperate regions of Argentina, Brazil, and Chile became the core areas for the European settlement by Germans, Italians, and Poles.

A new era in population movements was inaugurated by the voyages of discovery in the 15th and 16th centuries. Earlier migrations had been mainly overland or across land-locked seas. Oceans had been barriers; gradually they became highways. This oceanic period led to major changes of residence, predominantly over the waters, but with the restrictions and hindrances discussed above and with strong ties to church affiliations and previous occupancy.

Other new features were the enormous extent of the new lands and the weak power of resistance by earlier inhabitants. This new ability to traverse the oceans disturbed the equilibrium previously existing between different human groups and initiated currents of migration which grew in volume and spread from area to area.

Associated with these migrations was a sizeable and accelerating growth of the world population, increasing almost sevenfold since the middle of the 17th century. Europe was the chief instigator of these migrations, laying the groundwork for the big splash discussed in Chapter 1. Almost one-third of the earth's population today consists of Europeans by blood, most of whom are now living outside of that continent. There are also between six and seven times as many Europeans living elsewhere as were living in Europe in the 17th century. Europe itself has grown more than fivefold since then. Of Europeans living elsewhere, three-fifths are in the United States.

The new forms of movement following the period of discoveries and its transoceanic thrust have two phases: colonization and immigration. In colonization, states sent out their citizens to settle in new countries, frequently overseas. The motive was the commercial advancement of the recipient state by the taking over of administrative functions.

Immigration differed from colonization in principle, since it was not a state undertaking but resulted from spontaneous decisions by individuals. There has never been any appreciable migration between the temperate zones and the tropics, in either direction, nor have the polar regions ever been concerned. Practically all migration, historically speaking, has been between countries of the temperate zones. As a rule the country receiving the immigrants was less populated, and living conditions more favorable, as the ratio between population and land was low.

Population density is an index to the direction of the movement. The immigrant-receiving countries invariably show a small number of persons to the square mile (App. Table 8, Set A), contrasted with densely populated countries (Set B). In Europe the density of population (per square mile) rarely falls below 300 and it rises toward 1,000, while in Asia, China has 283 persons to the square mile; Japan, 740; and India, 453.

Special Types of Regular Migration

Food and population pressure explain several less dramatic movements of people. Nomadic pastoralists still exist both in Asia and tropical Africa; otherwise this pattern, which was common in man's early history, has vanished with settlement. Nomads roam over large expanses to find grazing grounds, often according to a strict seasonal pattern. An intermediary phenomenon which is slowly vanishing is transhumance; farmers in the lowlands and valleys of Scandinavia and Switzerland used to drive their cattle and sheep up the mountains for additional grazing in summertime. The return was more milk, largely converted into less perishable cheeses. The eastern Mediterranean and the Balkans still practice transhumance of this style during the dry, hot summer, taking refuge at higher altitudes, thereby obtaining food that otherwise would not have accrued. No hungry, poor people can afford to abandon this kind of subsistence.

A special kind of seasonal migration takes place in Africa, particularly in South Africa. As soon as the harvest is finished, the men seek jobs in adjacent or distant cities, relieving the direct feeding burden of the villages and allowing the earning of cash for food purchases. These phenomena are adjustments to a very parsimonious existence, and open a way to reduce the ravaging effects of hungry weeks. Studies of South African labor migration to mining districts (Muhlenberg,1976) have shown that the length of sojourn is determined by the size of the crops. In bad crop years migration to the cities not only starts earlier but is of much longer duration. There is a direct correlation between availability of food and the extent of the migration. In other words, the size of the feeding burden and the population pressure are decisive factors in this kind of migration.

In a strict sense, shifting cultivation may also be classified as migration enforced by the constraints of nature, when rainfall or soil structure necessitates a recurrent shift of land for tillage within a sequence of two to ten years.

Criteria for Overpopulation

Countries are often referred to as either overpopulated or under-populated. Between these two extremes lies a wide optimum range. In particular overpopulation has been given considerable attention, and there are several definitions associated with the term. An area is considered over-populated when (1) fewer people would lead to a higher level of living, or (2) if population increases are more rapid than possible production gains, or (3) if continuance of prevailing growth trends would check economic advances. Using the first definition, almost the entire world is overpopulated. Exceptions could possibly be countries such as Canada, Brazil, or the Congo. Using the second criteria, indications of overpopulation are less clear. But this second alternative requires amplification. As soon as disparities within countries are taken into account, many alarming trends are discovered. The true conditions are masked by seemingly satisfactory totals or even averages. Japan, Mexico, Brazil and several other countries show major sectors of their population lagging behind and not becoming a part of the market economy. These groups give evidence of dropping incomes, less adequate diets, and similar disadvantageous developments.

This lag factor — or history if one prefers that notion — may have a much deeper root. The analysis has to be made on a resource basis, with a *complete* accounting made. Advances too often have been gained by tapping forest lands, groundwater reserves, soils through erosion or depletion, or, still more insidiously, by a nutritional undermining that provides calories but creates serious protein, mineral, and vitamin imbalances.

In theory, population equilibrium could be measured many ways and be correspondingly defined. Such alternative gauges could be (1) life span, (2) fertility rate, (3) balance between birth and death rates, or (4) net growth. Other basic considerations would obviously be net migration (in or out), net trade, primarily in food and feed, and not the least important, the degree of water imbalance.

Another key factor is optimum rate of growth. Many countries of Latin America and Africa point to their untapped resources, not recognizing that what counts is the rate at which such slumbering assets can be mobilized. Equally crucial in relation to future numbers is the time factor. Will available resources, whether fuel (coal, petroleum), water, soil or forests, last for one decade or for one century at present growth rates? Such a breakpoint may well be reached in the present generation, within 25 to 30 years, or at best in the next century, in any case not a very reassuring prospect.

In highly industrialized countries the population can vary within wide limits without having a serious effect on the level of real income or other criteria of optima. Developing countries, however, lack such flexibility; for them the questions of overpopulation and underpopulation are extremely crucial.

Going one step further to what is basically a biological phenomenon, overpopulation exists whenever true self-sufficiency is faltering. Countries often hailed as economic miracles, such as the United Kingdom, the Netherlands, Italy, Germany, as well as Japan, emerge from such a biological scrutiny as very critical examples of overpopulation. A country should certainly be labelled as overpopulated when its own lands cannot feed more than a fraction of its resident population, when major proportions of its population have been lifted off to other countries or continents, or when agricultural production is not matching the total increase in numbers and no longer can sustain an adequate diet for all.

This entire line of reasoning raises the fundamental question of criteria. By radical shifts downward in nutritional standards, could these countries possibly provide for their people? In answering that query, a big question mark would be attached to such countries as Japan, the United Kingdom, the Netherlands, Italy, and many more. This speculation, however, is an exercise in theoretical futility. Overpopulation will always remain an imprecise, pragmatic term. Even so, one basic adjustment should be made; overpopulation should be given a clear biological connotation and not be mirrored in vague, economic abstractions. In all common sense a country is overpopulated when it has too many people to be supplied by the inadequate basic resources of its territory. (See further, p. 51-52.)

It is high time that biologists and geographers take a far more serious part in this debate. The oversimplification and misconceptions surrounding the food-and-people issue make such a renewed involvement urgent. This is in effect a research field with a long, reputable tradition, but which has been swamped in the euphoria of seeming progress. In retrospect it is a tragedy to mankind that this issue has become so seriously blurred by imprecise phraseology and enmeshed in alleged economic terms, which were either ill-defined or, still worse, formulated in a piecemeal manner, oblivious of the need for a total and global cost accounting.

The Foresight of Malthus

The British economist Thomas Robert Malthus pointed out the disparity between the possible growth of the population on the one hand, and the means of subsistence on the other; population growth follows a geometric progression, whereas the means of subsistence expand only through arithmetical progression. Benjamin Franklin also came close to formulating the very same principle, as did a Chinese scholar in the 18th century. They were both among the many forerunners to Malthus, whose famous *Essay on Population* was first published in 1798, and much expanded and revised in the second (1803) and subsequent editions.

Malthus' analysis has withstood the test of time. According to him, population grows geometrically and may, on the basis of that principle, double within 25 years. The principle was put forward as a possibility, but the author received confirmation in the case of the British colonies in North America, which enjoyed particularly favorable conditions for expansion. In contrast to population growth, food production can only increase arithmetically because of an indispensable added input, whether in soil, water, or minerals. This is merely a reformulation which fits nicely with the well-known law of diminishing returns.* Malthus' reminder of the harsh factors limiting man's numbers is equally valid. These assertions are almost axiomatic in nature and should really be above controversy and argument.

The disparity between the two rates of growth acts in itself as a natural brake on unlimited demographic growth; Malthus wished to substitute a voluntary regulatory mechanism for this natural one. To be more precise, he wished to substitute "preventive checks" for "positive checks." Those "positive checks" are wars and exceptional occurrences which are possible to avoid; but, in any case, the shortage of food constitutes the ultimate positive obstacle. Many of the "preventive checks" were rejected by Malthus, especially those termed vicious, such as adultery, prostitution and sexual deviation. Up to this point most would agree. Arguments arose when Malthus did not approve of either birth control or abortion as "preventive checks," accepting only "moral restraint" — prolonged celibacy, coupled with chastity.

Malthus was well aware of the possibilities of technical, agricultural and industrial progress and devoted sections of his study to such advances, known or still to come. He fully recognized the potentialities in this regard, even visualized the day when the whole globe would be "cultivated like a garden." His law still tends to be true. He was well acquainted with the new "promised lands" of the prairies and the pampas. The irony of history, however, is that this wealth fell to the white man, who thereby generated the fallacious belief that the earth could feed any number of people. Still worse, Western man thought he held the monopoly on infallible techniques to accomplish this task and the exclusive right to the riches.

Sandbagging the Human
Tidal Wave

The truth of the matter is that the present human population already is much greater than the earth can adequately maintain as free human beings, and there is no foreseeable method in which the exponential growth curve can be slowed in time to forestall disaster. Approximately two-thirds of the world's present population is undernourished, with hundreds of millions eking out an existence at the near-starvation level. The largest increases in population are occurring in precisely those areas where hunger is

---

* In relative terms it costs more and more to arrive at a fixed return, or, you are getting less and less in return for the identical amount of input.

most endemic (App. Table 10). Some of those populations are doubling in less than 25 years, resulting in a disproportionate preponderance of young people and the accompanying increase in child-bearing women.

The population issue affects all the peoples of the earth, rich and poor, the few and the numerous, those nations with ample resources and those without. The wealthy nations or those that can commandeer the resources of other nations may stave off Doomsday for a longer period than other countries, but they, too, are facing severe social and economic problems arising from population growth. The situation is such that a policy of strict population control is mandatory for the entire world, and such a policy must be effected shortly.

Obviously, the exponential growth in population gives rise to serious repercussions with food, resources, land, and the quality of life. Failure to tackle these issues will lead to catastrophe. Either the birth rate must fall or the death rate must rise. This dilemma cannot be talked away.

Currently, one-third of the world's population is satiated by consuming three-quarters of the earth's harvested crops. Ironically, the greatest increases in food production in the past decades have occurred in the Satisfied World (SW)*, not the Hungry World (HW). Agricultural science and technology flourish among the well-fed and languish among the hungry. As a result, the satiated are threatened with obesity, the hungry with starvation. In the United States farmers are paid not to grow certain crops in order to artificially maintain a price structure, a procedure which has precedence over feeding hungry people, including millions in the United States itself. Some surplus foods are prohibited from being shipped to hungry countries with whom there are ideological differences.

Reflecting — perhaps somewhat belatedly — the widespread concern over the exploding world population, the United Nations is to lead an international effort which will peak in 1974, designated the "World Population Year." Much of the money and some of the technical assistance for this global, educational, and investigatory project will be provided by the United Nations Fund for Population Activities. A working group which includes five non-governmental organizations, such as the International Planned Parenthood Federation, has been set up to coordinate the plan of attack.

The fundamental task is to obtain as complete and accurate statistics as is possible. To this end efforts will be made to encourage population censuses, better birth records, sample registration for population growth estimates, and fertility surveys. These will encompass knowledge about family planning, attitudes toward sexual matters, birth control practices, and contraceptive devices. Much of this work has already been launched. Several countries are planning demographic and population surveys, and

---

* The Satisfied World (SW) comprises those countries where the average per capita intake of food is above minimum requirements, primarily North America, Europe, the U.S.S.R., Australia, New Zealand, Japan, Argentina, and Uruguay.

the United Nations hopes to start a world fertility survey, spread over five years.

Apart from measuring the high water marks of the human tide, the United Nations has set itself the equally vital task of bringing home to the peoples of the world — at individual as well as governmental level — the dangers of their swelling numbers. Although by far the greatest increases will be in developing countries, only about one-third of the countries in this category have given their family planning programs national status. Further there is a critical shortage of trained experts on a global basis. Plans are therefore underway to set up a world population institute to provide the manpower for a continuing assault on the issue.

In bringing its message directly to the grass roots, the plan will rely on a decentralized approach, mobilizing help from wherever it is offered — foundations and charitable funds as well as communications media of all kinds. In light of the mounting crisis, several governments are reversing their attitudes and policies. Most dramatic is the recent 180-degree turnabout in Mexico, with the government giving full support to family planning efforts after decades of persistent opposition to all such undertakings.

Enlightenment on such a massive scale as proposed by the United Nations cannot fail to have an impact. Far too many governments and institutions are dragging their feet, and far too many economic and political leaders are playing "ostrich." The World Population Year will hopefully firm up the global efforts of man to regain control of his destiny by restraint on his procreating forces. If unchecked, most living organisms could ultimately cover the earth, but man supposedly has the unique capability of long-range thinking and planning and the ability to act thereon. Now is the time to give convincing evidence of those talents. The United Nations program could be a significant vehicle but must be brought into action programs. Coordinated and concomitant efforts are equally needed in a number of other areas. Population is but one of these, but a mighty decisive one!

Chapter 3

Postwar
Food Production

Currently, one-third of the human race disposes of two-thirds of the food and feed production from both land and water. Nine-tenths of the world's food (measured in calories) is in vegetable products, of which four-fifths constitutes starchy foods, such as grains or tubers (potato, sweet potato, cassava, yams, and others). Contrary to many publicized views, most food and feed originate with agriculture and fisheries. Synthetic foods represent a mere trifle in global terms, and industrially manufactured vitamins are almost exclusively channelled to the well-fed world and to its livestock.

Global Food Production

The most remarkable feature of food production during the past quarter-century is the astonishing progress made in increasing the volume from both agriculture and fisheries. Cereal production, for instance, shows a gain of more than a half-billion tons, far ahead of the concomitant percentage increase in human numbers: 73 per cent as against 49.5 per cent.

The greatest achievements in food production are the significant expansions in tilled acreage in the Soviet Union and China, involving almost 100 million acres in each country and enlarging grain production by 91 and 85 million metric tons respectively. In the U.S.S.R. the new grain baskets in western Siberia and Kazakhstan account for most of this expansion; in China it was achieved through the irrigation drive. These feats are mirrored in the continental data which show the relative share of these larger outputs. In absolute terms they reveal that Asia demonstrates a gain almost three times that of Europe and twice that of the Soviet Union. On the other hand Africa and Latin America exhibit increases less than half as large as those of

Europe. On such an overall basis cereals have run ahead of population everywhere, with Africa the closest (App. Table 11).

A major portion of the increase in cereals is in the category of feed grains to the Satisfied World (SW). With the exception of China, however, animal production has had a poor showing in the Hungry World. (HW). At

Commodities — Global Gains in Production
(in million metric tons)

	1948-52	Annual average 1969-70	Per Cent Gain
Total cereals	692.1	1,197.5	73
- Wheat	171.2	311.6	82
- Rice	167.3	306.8	84
- Corn	139.8	266.8	92
- Millet and Sorghum	47.8	92.5	93
Legumes	29.3	44.4	51.5
Potato	247.4	299.5	22
Sweet Potato	69.4	142.3	105
Sugar	37.8	84.7	124
Oilseeds	51.6	108.6	112
Milk	258.4	399.4	54
Meat (excl. poultry, horse)	41.0	80.4	96
Eggs	10.2	20.4	100
Fish and Shellfish	21.7	63.0	190
World Population (million)	2,497.6	3,722.1	49.5

Source: FAO Production Yearbook 1970

the same time, the per capita crop production in the HW has not kept pace with the population figures as has occurred in the SW (App. Table 9). These data mask the fact that if the present human population were to be provided with the minimum quantities considered essential by modern nutritional standards, current food production in the HW actually would have to double. Global rationing would consequently lead to universal hunger. Percentages generally indicate different amounts when referring to high intakes. For instance, many of the gains in Africa and Latin America fall in the category of export crops. Percentages are also deceptive when there are fluctuations between years and even more deceptive when considerable economic discrepancies prevail within a country. Gains then tend to favor a privileged minority.

Equally deceptive are volume data when unrelated to population figures. China is a colossus with one-fifth (23.4%) of the world's population. It dominates world agricultural production in several crops and livestock categories, among them rice, sweet potato, soybeans, and pork

(App. Table 12). But this dominance is mainly by sheer numbers. Per capita there are several countries with a far higher production rate. What counts is the actual amount of food available for each individual, and what shows is a general failure to take care of the 2,000 millions added to the globe since 1900.

Crop Production

Cereals, almost exclusively domesticated grasses, have been grown for thousands of years and are consumed as bread or unleavened cakes, such as East Indian chapattis or Mexican tortillas. Food and feed cereals of various kinds are grown in almost every country on earth. Rice is the chief staple for half the world's population and constitutes as much as 80 per cent of the calories for most of Asia's peoples. Wheat ranks second to rice in worldwide use but is the principal cereal of North America and parts of Europe. Corn dominates as food in Latin America and parts of Africa, and as feed in the United States, Argentina, and South Africa.

In addition to cereals, legumes are also important sources of protein (complementary to that of cereals) in several parts of the world. Soybeans in various forms such as meal and curd have long been basic to the Orient, and the groundnut (peanut) and locust bean are used widely as protein sources in many parts of Africa. Beans are justly given the designation of the poor man's meat, "carne de pobre" in Spanish, "carne di poveri" in Italian.

The American Indians discovered the wholesome effect of combining corn with beans, a practice which is still the dominant pattern all over Latin America, especially in Mexico, Brazil, and Peru, but also in Italy and other Mediterranean regions. India also grows and uses a great number of beans (Bengal gram, red gram, cow peas, kidney beans, and others).

No further review will be made of the innumerable seeds, leaves, tubers, stems, shoots, or flowers which may be used as food. As for fruits and vegetables, they are mainly a source of vitamins and minerals and provide invaluable roughage to the bowel functions.

Many tubers constitute a good source of calories. The ordinary white potato, for example, has written economic and social history because of its high nutritive value. In quantity potato is comparable to cereals, but in nutritive quality it is far superior.

Production Gains. Gains in crop production are primarily due to expanded areas of cultivation, yet the soils in these areas are generally less suitable for cropping than those previously tilled. Gain in yield (production per unit area) is a characteristic feature of the SW and a few countries or regions of the HW. Double-cropping, mostly combined with irrigation and a larger use of appropriate fertilizers, has allowed higher outputs in parts of the Philippines, in India, Indonesia, South Korea, Pakistan and Taiwan.

Gains in Crop Production
and Yields Per Acre 1948-52 to 1969-70

	Production Per Cent Increase	Yield Per Acre Per Cent Increase
Wheat	82	49
Rice	84	39
Corn	92	51
Millet and Sorghum	93	61
Potato	21	21
Sweet Potato and Yams	105	26

Only since 1968 has the so-called Green Revolution initiated a trend toward greater returns per acre. The actual results have been less than generally assumed since in most of the involved countries 40 to 60 per cent of the gains are to be ascribed to expanded acreages. Only in two instances, namely wheat in India and Mexico, have yields per acre managed to outrun population gains, a feat accomplished chiefly through irrigation. For a time rice yields were ahead in Ceylon but lagged behind population growth in 1970. This is not surprising; the Asian countries involved in the Green Revolution have added almost one-quarter billion people in the 1960's and are expected to add some 300 million in the 1970's and close to a half-billion by 1985. These numbers provide an immense order of foodstuffs to fill.

Many sweeping and misleading statements are made about agricultural conditions in "developing" countries, a term which in itself is fallacious. In general it is assumed that agricultural production in these areas is universally neglected and that yields fall far behind those of "developed" countries. Such examples undoubtedly exist, but there are many instances in which the reverse is true (App. Table 13).

Gains versus Population Growth. As indicated earlier, cereal production has grown by no less than a half-billion metric tons in the last 20 years, a growth primarily prompted by cultivation of additional millions

Cereal Grains
Gains in Production and Acreages
1948-52 to 1968-71

	SW	HW
Million metric tons	+59.3	+446.1
Million acres	-61.8	+291.5

acres. The rich countries show a drop of 62 million acres but have compensated by displaying higher yields. In the poor countries the yields have had a much smaller rise. The Soviet Union and China account for the greatest gains in annual volume despite setbacks in climatically critical years.

No unused arable land is available in the Middle East, which houses some 75 million people, but a possible 5 million acres may be added through harnessing every remaining water resource. With a projection of 50 million people to be added by 1985, however, this measure will accommodate merely a fraction of the expected increase in human beings.

In 1975, when the Aswan Dam is planned to be in full operation, it is expected that the food production of Egypt will have increased 35 per cent since work on the dam began. But in the meantime the population will have risen by no less than 48 per cent. Latin America has an equally alarming situation. Its population will exceed 650 million before year 2000, yet this continent only is adequately feeding less than one-half of its present 300 million inhabitants. Among major countries Mexico has an exceedingly high birth rate, 3.3 per cent, and is adding almost 2 million people each year. At this rate it will exceed 100 million people in year 2000. Brazil, presently growing by almost 3 million annually and barely balancing this increase out by comparable gains in acreages or yields, is just attaining the 100 million figure.

Animal Production

Milk has remained largely a feature of the Western world (App. Table 14), while in the HW, milk is of significance in only a few areas with lengthy nomadic tradition, such as Mongolia, Mauritania, and Somalia. This limited use of milk is closely connected with lactose intolerance which is presumably genetically determined and is characteristic of many peoples in the warm world, such as Asians, most Africans, and American Indians. Almost one-third of the protein produced through milk is channelled into the feeding of calves and other young, or deliberately wasted. For example, whey, a by-product of cheese-making, contains high-rated proteins which are only partially saved.

The production of meat protein is nearly seven times greater in the developed world than in the developing regions. Some 40 countries produce and also consume the bulk of the world's meat supply. (Fig. 1). The United States (25.8%), followed by the Soviet Union (12.0%), Argentina (6.5%), China (5.6%), Brazil (4.8%) and France (4.2%) dominate beef production. Australia (11.8%) and the Soviet Union (11.3%) lead in mutton and lamb, followed by China (8.8%) and New Zealand (8.2%). Pork is prevalent in Asia and Europe, each with one-third of the total. But China is the largest pork-producing country (24%), not on a commercial basis, but exclusively for subsistence. Furthermore, hogs in China are scavengers, in effect acting as sewage plants. Poultry is similarly raised on waste and weeds. In the SW beef is increasingly being fattened on feed crops and less on grazing pastures and rangelands. Feeding operations based on mixtures

Global Meat Production, 1969-71

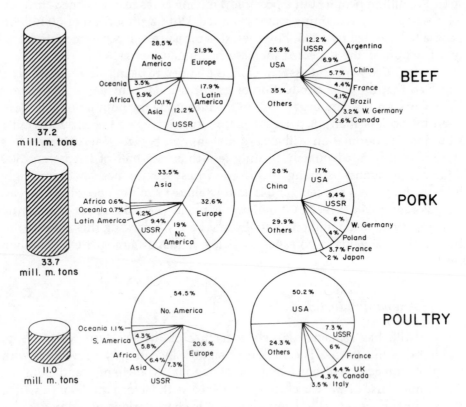

Figure 1: Global meat production, by continents and by selected countires.

supplemented by amino acids, vitamins, and minerals, have made both hog- and poultry-raising highly efficient enterprises in the developed countries.

Western countries dominate the world market for poultry and eggs, but Japan has surged to third rank in egg output. (App. Table 14). In both cases this increased production is based on supplementary fish meal from distant oceans and on soybeans, corn, millet, and other feed from the North American prairie, Africa and Thailand.

Fisheries

The advance in fisheries during the postwar period has been still greater than in agriculture (see table on p. 30). Ocean catches have grown almost threefold. In order to sustain a high level of animal production, however, almost half the marine harvest moves as fish meal into the feeding troughs of the affluent world. This situation is reflected in the far greater postwar gains in feed fish as compared to fish used directly for human consumption.

Gains in Ocean Catches
(in million metric tons)

	1948-52 to 1969-70	*1959-60 to 1969-70*
Food fish	12.5	6.3
Feed fish	20.5	15.6

The trend is unmistakable. More and more of the ocean harvest is being shunted away from man to livestock, pets, and fur animals. Despite all the technological advances, little is being done to remedy this trend — not the least of our tragedies. The facetious observation that people have been forgotten in man's ocean pursuits or have been relegated to second-class customers seems justified. The catchwords, "Freedom from Hunger," have certainly been given a very quaint interpretation. Hogs, chickens, and pets of the well-to-do, living in the shadow of their rich purveyors, have never had it so good. People — in particular needy people — rate very low in this game of preferentials, as the riches of the oceans are withheld from them.

The catching of fish for human consumption also is firmly controlled by the rich nations. Since the 1950's the Soviet Union, Japan, and Europe have been involved in a large-scale deployment of newly built, mammoth fishing vessels, serviced by equally modern floating canneries. This dazzling thrust involves all oceans and encompasses most of the world's remaining fishing grounds. Few poor, hungry countries can afford to match these capital and fuel expenditures. They have been priced out of sharing the ocean's riches.

The most ominous aspect of this grand-scale grab of ocean riches is that this thrust is relentlessly pursued by a constant flow of new ships, when existing fleets are entirely capable of doubling the present global catches. In the name of economics, this raises an urgent plea for some kind of international planning or regulation of ocean fishing operations.

Aquatic Protein Underrated. Despite these crucial aberrations it is important to remember that to more than one billion people, fish bridges the gap between starvation and subsistence. In addition fish provides more protein than does beef (6.1 million metric tons as against 5.8 in 1969-70), and in many hungry countries aquatic protein dominates the intake of animal protein (App. Table 15). Despite recent efforts in Japan to switch to a Western diet, more than half of its animal protein intake is attributed to fish and shellfish. In addition, a major part of its animal production is based on fish meal. Fish is highly important to most countries of the Far East and surprisingly to tropical Africa also. It is relatively less important in Europe, where Portugal and Iceland lead the parade.

Ocean Crutches. Still more important is the question of how the oceans rate in comparison to agriculture. Several years ago this author introduced the concept of *fish acreage* by calculating the amount of tilled land required in each individual country to produce a corresponding amount of animal protein through feed crops. Looking at the globe in such terms, we discover that Japan would need to almost triple its tilled land. In other words, the ocean harvest represents close to three Japans. For many Western countries the figures are almost as dramatic. For instance, even in the Netherlands, where the soil is highly productive, the fish acreage represents 1.5 times the area of tilled land. So extravagant and frivolous are the Netherlanders that they give their livestock 7 times more fish protein than they themselves consume as seafood. The fish acreage figure for West Germany is 71 per cent, and for Portugal, 68 per cent of the tilled land. It is more widely acknowledged, however, that Portugal is dependent on the oceans. England shows 70 per cent fish acreage and Italy, 19.5.* On the Chinese scene, fish protein is equivalent to one-fifth of the tilled land.

Synthetic Food

Synthetic food, a term often broadened into covering the cultivation of microbes for use in bacterial croquettes, algal soups, and yeast cheeses, has played almost no role in the postwar period, never having reached sufficient production volume to be significant in world feeding. Both truly synthetic foods as well as these microbial products are founded on raw material and substrates which originate in green plant production, current or fossil (oil, coal, etc.). Another field consists entirely of foods made from plant products which imitate animal products (meat, milk, eggs, and others), thereby circumventing costly conversion; however, this area so far is limited in scope and is largely a phenomenon of affluent countries. The HW needs no such imitation as it already has carried on this basic switch through products of its own, best evidenced in the innumerable foods made from soybeans, peanuts, coconuts, etc. and constituting part of its daily diet. Both milks and cheeses (curds) are made from plant sources.

Global Calorie and Protein Budget

Approximately two-thirds (69%) of the protein consumption in the world is presently derived from plants. Pulses, although a smaller crop than cereals, play a significant role in complementing cereal protein. One-third of the world's protein originates with animals, and close to one-fifth takes the form of aquatic protein. The more populated that countries become, the

* All these data refer to 1969/70.

more they are forced to economize with soil resources and to depend directly on crops for protein, by-passing food-producing animals.

The food-and-people ratio is directly reflected in the nutritional standard. Technical advances in food production have done surprisingly little in changing this rule, although climate and other related agricultural constraints are and always have been supremely dictatorial. Only trade has upset this bondage in any decisive way, and then only by temporarily removing such hindrances in time and space.

A switch toward greater plant dependence creates difficulties in composing the diet and its processing. This is best evidenced by the far higher percentage for animal products in the protein budget of many regions as compared to their standing in caloric terms.

The Percentage Role of Plant and Animal Products in the Intake of Calories and Protein

	Calories		Protein	
	Plant	Animal	Plant	Animal
WORLD	90	10	69	31
Far East	94	6	86	14
- Japan	86	14	59	41
Middle East	82	12	85	15
Africa	93	7	84	16
Latin America	85	15	75	25
- Argentina	60	40	42	58
Western Europe	78	22	36	64
U.S.S.R.	80	20	61	39
North America	64	36	27	73
Australia & New Zealand	58	42	32	68

An additional complication is that most plant products require processing (milling, fermentation, cooking) in order to break up the indigestible cell walls and make their contents available for gastric utilization.

The nutritional dimension of food production can be shown by examining per capita protein intake. For instance, Mexico shows a deterioration in its nutritional standard, reflected by a drop in per capita intake of animal protein. The Mexicans have partially compensated for this lack by switching back to the traditional corn (tortilla) and bean diet. Presumably the situation is worse, as tourists are given priority for the available steaks. Tourist consumption is normally not subtracted in calculating national statistics.

Mexico — Per Capita Intake of Protein in Grams Per Day

	Cereals	Pulses	Plant Protein	Animal Protein	Meat	Milk	Eggs	Fish
1957-59	32.1	12.5	46.9	19.7	8.2	8.2	1.9	1.1
1964-66	35.9	14.0	52.1	14.2	6.9	5.4	1.1	0.8
Change	+3.8	+1.5	+5.2	-5.5	-1.3	-2.8	-0.8	-0.3

India constitutes a more critical case than Mexico as there is no margin of animal products on which to nibble. There is also a decline in the traditional intake of all kinds of beans, an indispensable nutritive supplement to cereal proteins. This drop has become even more serious as the Green Revolution boosted the relative availability and intake of cereals, thus worsening the delicate balance between grains and beans.

India — Per Capita Intake of Protein in Grams Per Day

	Cereals	Beans	Total Plant Protein	Animal Protein
1954-56	28.1	14.1	43.2	6.0
1969-70	31.6	10.8	43.8	5.6
Change	+3.5	-3.3	+0.6	-0.4

Limiting Factors in Global Food Production

Most discussions related to food production devote prime attention to factors that are conducive to higher yields per acre. This is logical and quite understandable when faced with the massively growing needs. Nonetheless this carries three major risks. Public debate and professional attention become focused on methods, each very circumscribed within its sphere and for this very reason far removed from realities manifest in the constraints — in the shape of clearly limiting factors — which are operative in several key regards. Secondly, few appraisals are made of costs as reflected in depleted or eroded soils, irreversibly tapped groundwater resources, deforested lands, and in disturbed ecological relationships hitting back through the spread of diseases. As a consequence no balanced account is ever presented, merely fragments in the form of positive accounts listing credit items but neglecting the debit posts. Thirdly, the raising of food is a huge biological operation exposed not only to the vagaries of the climate but also to the persistent assault from man's competitors (pests, diseases, weeds). Still to this very day few good statistics have been collected which measure the actual and regular losses in man's struggle for survival.

Constraints of Crop Production

Agricultural yields are determined by factors such as soil fertility, topography, water availability, climate, and input of energy, fertilizers, and spray chemicals. Since the HW is largely located in warm latitudes, the climate is a serious handicap. Higher evaporation means that the net return from rain and irrigation is correspondingly less. The soils of the tropics are generally of poorer quality; they contain less organic matter and fewer minerals, making them highly erosive. In the humid tropics the erosion is coupled with excessive leaching. Only be a shifting cultivation (slash-and-burn technique), which allows a rest period between turns in tillage, can the topsoil be sustained in these regions. It is becoming increasingly difficult, however, ot carry on such fallow as the pressure of mounting numbers requires permanent use of all land. In tropical Africa at least 250 million acres of tropical forest have disappeared in this way. In Asia 20 million acres, and in Latin America 15 to 25 million acres of forest have been similarly destroyed.

Erosion of the topsoil has reached seriously damaging dimensions on around 15 per cent of the world's agricultural lands. Another 15 per cent suffer from erosion coupled with critical mineral depletion. In many countries these losses are even higher. In the Philippines 75 per cent of the farmland is regularly damaged by erosion from torrential rains. In Somalia nine-tenths of all farmlands are reported to be eroded or threatened. More than half of India's soil is affected by such serious erosion that within 25 years the topsoil will have vanished on one-fourth of the tilled land. In 1957 it was estimated that water and wind erosion damaged about one-fourth of the total cultivated land in Argentina, and those losses have continued. In many regions of the world, overgrazing and excessive plowing have paved the way for destructive soil erosion, raising the need for restrictions both in tillage and animal raising.

Approximately one-third of the globe's land surface is grassland or cropland, one-third is forested, and the remainder is barren or otherwise unusable. Little change is predicted for the remainder of this century except for a net loss of 4.5 per cent in forested land area and the conversion of an estimated half of the present forests to grasslands or croplands. This move brings agriculture in direct conflict with forestry, although since the dawn of history there has been a battle between the ax and the plow. The net gain in tilled land has been considerably less than the forest-cleared lands. The price tag in disturbed climate and water balances has been high, but it has been even higher in eroded soils. Hopefully, man has learned a lesson.

The opening of new land will require considerable amounts of capital to reach, clear, irrigate, or fertilize it before it can reasonably produce food. The Food and Agriculture Organization (FAO) reports that these procedures are no longer economically feasible, despite the current pressing needs for food. In southern Asia, parts of eastern Asia, the Near East and North Africa, and in many sections of Latin America and tropical Africa there is almost no scope for expanding the arable area. As indicated earlier, to increase the production on land now in use is the only realistic proposal. Mankind has blazed its last trail and is putting an end to its horizontal thrust. It has been forced into a vertical build-up or intensification of new food resources, a kind of skyscraper recourse. No wonder one-fourth of the world's peoples now belong in the category of squatters, to which the grave urban dimension has been added.

We discover another area here in urgent need of coordination. Major regions of the poor world that once carried flourishing civilizations are overdeveloped and desperately short of forest lands. Who is going to yield to the soaring demands for food on the one hand, and for timber, paper and fuel, on the other? Furthermore, modern forestry is operating under the same spell of energy euphoria as agriculture. The current raiding of untapped forest resources in the warm belt for the benefit of a select few in Japan and the Western world is outrageous to a world battling for its survival.

Close to one-sixth of the world's soils are organic and have a limited lifespan. Soil scientists are trying to find ways of slowing down the depletion process which is insidiously destroying these rich, invaluable soils. Such soils need drainage, but this too often accelerates their destruction, a development which threatens to terminate conventional farming over vast areas of the globe. For example, in Florida soil breakdown takes place at the rate of one foot every year.

Statistically, each world inhabitant has at his disposal close to one acre (0.96 acre) of tilled land and two acres of grasslands for the raising of food and feed (App. Table 16). Each American citizen depends on 1.7 acres of tilled land. The net export of food and feed, represents another 0.4 acres potentially available to him. In addition, he requires 3.2 acres of rangeland or pasture. The Soviet Union has somewhat more tilled land per capita, but only half the pastureland acreage per person.

Acres Per Capita of the Four Most Populous Countries, 1960-70

	Tilled Land	Grassland
United States	2.1 (1.7)	3.2
U.S.S.R.	2.4	1.6
China	.33	.52
India	.32	.07
World	.96	2.0

Land shortage is frustrating an overwhelming number of farmers around the globe, most of whom are subsistence farmers. Yet these self-sustaining farmers — they can be counted in the hundreds of millions — on the average are short on one-third of the food and feed they need. They have to be content with "farms," more correctly termed "lots," which re only one to two acres in size. Furthermore, these are often fragmented into several minor holdings. Hence the clamor for more land has developed into various kinds of land reforms. Almost no country that has entered into such programs, highly justified from the social point of view, has adequate acreages to fill the demand, even with rigorous ceilings on the size of holdings.

The Irrigation Drive and
Ensuing Complications

Shortage of water is the most limiting factor in world agriculture; however, this century can indeed be called "the century of irrigation." Artificially watered acreage has been increased fourfold since 1900, with a further doubling assured through present projects prior to the year 2000. Some dams will serve 10 to 12 million acres, yet not provide food for more than 20 to 25 million on an Asian level. Since this is less than one year's population increment in Asia or two years in India, our technical feats operate on a time dimension different from that of the population tide. And a great dam these days takes almost 20 years to build! (App. Table 17).

Countries such as India, Bangladesh and China, where together more than one-third of the human race lives, are ruled by the vagaries of the monsoons. Some years these are insufficient, and occasionally they provide no rain at all. The dams are then not adequately filled. Although China and India together have the overwhelming share of the world's irrigated land (78%), they are both at the mercy of water shortage. At best dams can only ease a single-year drought.

As dams have grown higher (by several hundred feet) and reservoirs larger to accommodate year-round irrigation, a series of complications have arisen. These include the accelerated spread of water-borne diseases (a dry spell previously eliminated vectors or intermediary agents), increased losses through evaporation, extended salination, greater silt accumulation, and tilted seismic balances. The parasitic disease schistosomiasis has consistently spread up the Nile Valley and threatens the entire Egyptian population. Lately China battled this same infliction, having extended irrigation on a less than prudent scale. In Africa the Volta Dam caused a similar outbreak.

Salination is also a main battlefront in man's fight for food, requiring installations to drain away the salty water to avoid steadily mounting losses of tilled land. Currently, one-third of the Nile water now available for irrigation is used to remove salt, and this percentage is increasing. Glib talk about desalting ocean water for use in food production is particularly unrealistic. On top of the enormous energy amounts required to move water up and over the continental expanses come the salt residues. The amount of water involved make the logistics of this process prohibitive, not to mention the disposal of tons of salt per acre-foot of water.

Another factor reducing the net advantage of irrigation dams is the direct loss of land and the ensuing complex resettlements. Feeding canals and ditches permanently reduce the effectively watered acreage, often by one-fourth. In many cases very little consideration has been given to the lost "benefits" of annual floods which distributed fertile silt over large areas. It is often difficult and costly to substitute for this natural distribution through fertilizers.

Massive Input of Commercial Fertilizers

Under the pressure of growing human numbers, global crop production for both food and feed is persistently being pushed to higher levels through a massive input of chemicals for fertilizing, spraying, and fuel.

Until the 1960's less than one-eighth of the world's commercial fertilizers reached developing countries (Table 18 and the table below) and once there, were largely channelled to plantation crops for export purposes (sugar, bananas, coffee, and others). A similarly imbalanced distribution of resources applies to other agricultural chemicals.

In terms of nutrients (N, P_2O_5 and K_2O),* the current global input of commercial fertilizers exceeds the level of 70 million metric tons. The annually transported volume is more than twice that amount. It appears unlikely that even the developed world can afford to pursue this trend much further and aim for a sustained increase in production per acre. Man is approaching a point where this freight load comes close to the total weight of the human race. The persistent demand for higher yields — engendered by more people — spirals this flow of nutrients still further upward, and in turn raises the level of removal through the crops. In order to avert depletion it is vital to compensate for these mineral losses. The restoration, repair, and maintenance of the soils merely uphold the level of production and do not elevate the returns in higher yields per acre.

Fertilizer Use (NPK)   (in million metric tons)

	SW	HW	Total
1955-57	20.8	2.5	23.2
1965-67	38.9	6.8	45.7
1970-71	54.0	14.1	68.1
1975*	75.9	22.5	99.4
1980*	100.2	33.3	133.5

* Estimated

More than 800 million people on earth are already on this bandwagon and are directly dependent on the large machinery of fertilizer plants and on a network of delivery channels. While few studies have analyzed the full implications of these trends, there are several danger signs related to the excessive use of nitrogen, resulting in pollution of drainage water leading into rivers, lakes, and ponds, affecting drinking water and accumulating on leafy vegetables.

Advanced regions such as Europe and Japan have obtained a breakthrough in agricultural production through fertilization. Japan applies 48 times as much fertilizer nutrients per cultivated acre as India and twice that of Denmark. Per person Japan uses 8.5 times more than India.

* N = Nitrogen, P_2O_5 = Phosphate, K_2O = Potassium

Use of Commercial Fertilizers, in Nutrients, 1969-70

NPK Kg/capita		NPK Kg/acre	Population density Ares per capita*
2.6	India	3.4	30.2
3.9	China	11.8	13.2
10.9	Mexico	9.0	46.8
22.3	Japan	162.5	7.2
32.4	U.S.S.R.	13.8	95.6
71.7	U.S.A.	33.0	86.0
118.0	Denmark	86.4	54.4

* One are = 0.025 acre.

Despite the massive input of fertilizers, the expansion of double-cropping, and a far more favorable and dependable rainfall, Japan has failed to feed its people and has been forced to extend its subsistence by relying on imports of food from the huge acreages in the North American prairie, Australia, Thailand, and New Zealand. In addition, Japan has forcefully dipped into the ocean riches, consuming almost one-sixth of the ocean catches.

It is not only the amount of nutrients per acre that counts but also a balanced ratio of nitrogen, phosphate and potassium. In Japan it is 1:1:1 as against 1:0.24:0.15 in India, where soils have become exhausted by centuries of cultivation. To restore fertility and procure higher yields (as in the Green Revolution), it is necessary to bring in 40 to 70 per cent of both major and minor mineral nutrients through fertilizers. It is far from adequate to provide nitrogen only.

All this is brought out to emphasize that India could not possibly match an input of fertilizers of Japanese dimensions. To achieve a similar per capita input, India would need annually an added 11.5 million metric tons, but on an acreage basis would require 65.5 million metric tons. The first figure is one-sixth of the present total world consumption and the second almost identical to entire global use. The monsoon irregularities also make it highly unlikely that India could accommodate any such enormous quantities. Where perennial irrigation with multi-cropping is practiced, this level of mineral input makes the risks for salt accumulating (salination) far greater.

Hazards of Animal Production

In the HW yields of meat and milk are low both per animal and per unit area of pastures. Only areas which cannot be cultivated are used for pastures, and they often turn desolate and barren from overgrazing and water shortage. Since capital for fertilizing pastures is scarce, the forage is frequently low in protein and minerals. To import feed as is the practice in eastern and western Europe is beyond the economic reach of the HW. Because of such deficiencies, livestock and poultry are low-yielding, and diseases and parasites are prevalent.

The well-to-do world has become increasingly dependent on the raising of feed crops for its animal production, often devoting more tilled land to this purpose than to food crops; however, few countries in the HW could allocate their scanty resources of tilled land for such purposes. The alternative, resorting to grazing animals, has limited chances for two basic reasons. Pasture lands persistently have had to yield to the plow, to the limit in key areas. In some regions the point of ecological prudence has been passed, as in India where pasturelands in acreages constitute only seven per cent of the tilled land. This also happened in our own dry prairies resulting in the Dust-Bowl catastrophes in 1924 and 1935, but in contrast to India we with our ample land resources could take such tolls. Few remaining grasslands in the HW allow high-level production. Instead it is likely that nomadism or varying types of transhumance will recur.

Determinism in Full Reign

The debate and controversy that raged in geography a quarter of a century ago between determinists and possibilists largely evaded basic distinctions. Both sides failed to recognize that wherever there are human settlements, living beings have to be provided with an adequate basis for survival. That is, people have to be fed and furnished with water, housing and clothing. The Saharan oil villages or the Canadian and Soviet mining towns in the Arctic prove little, even do next to nothing in removing or affecting the obvious geographical constraints. Rather they can be compared to ocean liners. Like the millions in cities, their survival hinges on land. Even though located at considerable distances away, they must be supported by a vast transportation net which continually grows in size and complexity and widens into gigantic transfers of food, water and fuel oil. The deterministic factors are still in full play, perhaps even more so since the vulnerability index has been climbing continuously.

The complete escape from reality is symbolized by such technical adventurism as talk of growing food on the moon, on top of Mount Everest, or in aquatic farms on the bottom of the ocean. All cost considerations are thrown overboard while feasibility studies reign supremely, detached from accountability.

Center Stage

How to feed the world's growing population will be an excruciating predicament for many years to come. Mankind does not lack the potential for increasing world food production, but it is not likely that this potential will be realized in time. Achieving a satisfactory balance between food and people will require dramatic increases in farm productivity in Asia, Africa, and Latin America, where more than half of the world's populations reside.

Such presumptive gains, however, will be futile unless effective brakes are put on population growth. Present trends need to be reversed if we wish to provide a decent living for a majority of the human family and to move into the 21st century with a reasonable chance of true progress. Producing more food is ineffectual if coordinated and drastic measures are not taken to improve storage, processing, and marketing. It is not very clever to feed still more rats, insects, and foraging birds, depriving man of his hard-earned victuals. Gross National Waste should be given as much attention as Gross National Product and be balanced in a reasonable manner.

More food needs to be tailored to fit nutritional requirements. The world, if it so desires, can easily acquire more calories through starch, sugar and even fats, but proteins, calcium, and vitamins of the A, B, and E groups are critically short. There are overwhelming indications that if protein is adequate, disease resistance is enhanced in both man and livestock. For the same reason trace elements are crucial to protect plants against microbial attacks.

Superimposed upon all these shortcomings is the need to formulate a strategy introducing the biological dimension to both technology and economics. This is an exciting challenge that centers around the prudent use of both renewable and non-renewable resources. Soils, water, minerals, and energy will be the key elements of this endeavor. Most important, this will mean placing the food-and-people dilemma at center stage.

Chapter 4

Man's Dominion

Biologists have far too long been playing the numbers' game of demographers and economists. The French entomologist Fabre made the astute observation that scientists must teach man how to count *himself*. We have poorly addressed ourselves to this onerous task. In biological terms man is far more than a statistic. He is a solar system of living organisms — his biological dominion — and to be counted within this immediate biosphere of man are livestock of all kinds, used for both food and as a labor force for the hauling of burdens or the threshing of grain. Thus on the basis of sheer weight, man and livestock can be placed on a commensurate basis of sorts. In this case the plant kingdom has a feeding burden that is not the one per cent so frequently quoted but actually five to six times higher.

A more accurate way to place man and animal on a commensurate basis is to compare their intake of primary plant protein. This is a kind of biological rating. In such terms the earth is inhabited by more than just 3.78 billion humans (1972). To maintain man's present nutritional standards and to retain the type of agriculture now prevailing, plant crops and grazing lands must carry a feeding burden far in excess of the human numbers. The biosphere, in the form of livestock (poultry included) that is required to keep the human biomass going, adds up to a protein consumption corresponding to that of 14.4 billion people. This figure is computed on the basis of an average man (70 kg = 154 lbs.), who requires a daily protein intake of 70 grams (= 2½ oz.). Consequently, within man's direct dominance there are 18 billion population equivalents (PE units) in operation. (See Borgstrom, *The Hungry Planet*, Chapter 1.)

Continental Ratios of Livestock to Man

The above computation renders a global ratio between livestock and man of 4.0 (Fig. 2). Asia shows slightly more than half that figure, reflecting

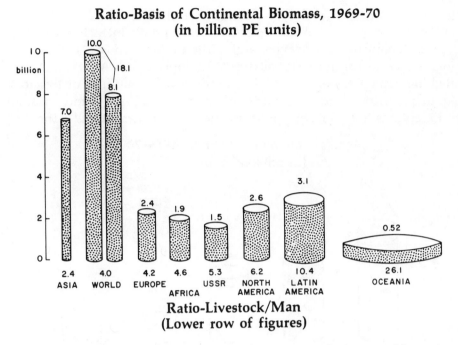

Ratio-Basis of Continental Biomass, 1969-70
(in billion PE units)

Ratio-Livestock/Man
(Lower row of figures)

Figure 2: The ratio Livestock to Man, by continents (bottom set of figures).

its more narrow margin. The biological pressure of Asia is high already in terms of man himself (2.08 billion), but in terms of PE units, it is far greater, namely 7 billion, of which the livestock represents 4.9 billion PE units. This situation weighs down the world ratio heavily.

Continental Biomass, 1969-70
(in billion PE units)

	Man	Livestock	Total	Ratio Livestock/Man
Asia	2.08	4.89	6.97	2.3
WORLD	3.65	14.47	18.12	3.9
Europe	0.46	1.92	2.38	4.2 (2.5)
Africa	0.34	1.71	2.05*	4.6
U.S.S.R.	0.24	1.32	1.56	5.5
North America	0.225	1.39	1.62	6.2
Latin America	0.275	2.85	3.13	10.3
Oceania	0.016	0.496	0.51	31.1

* Adjusted for imported grain.

Asia has four times as many people as Europe but only two and a half times as much livestock. Compared to North America, Asia has nine times more people and three and a half times more livestock.

Overpopulated Europe enjoys a surprisingly comfortable ratio of 4.2, because some two-fifths of Europe's livestock is fed from external sources. When this circumstance is taken into account, Europe's ratio is adjusted downward to a level very close to that of Asia, or 2.5.

Africa stays close to the world average, a ratio which clearly refutes the notion about the top-heaviness of cattle in Africa (Fig. 3). There are biological reasons for this ratio; outside of Ethiopia, South Africa, and some limited highland areas of East Africa, conditions for all kinds of livestock are quite precarious, and the ratio is only half that of Asia, namely around one. Exceptions are nomadic countries such as Mauritania and Somalia.

Man's Dominion in Africa, 1969-70
(in million PE units)

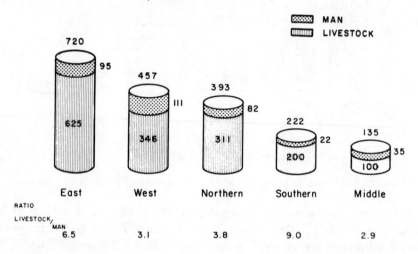

Figure 3: Man's Dominion measured in human population and livestock for the major regions of Africa. Note the emptiness of the center of the continent, and the dominance of the East as compared to the West, and the equal balance between North and South.

The Soviet Union and North America enjoy the greatest soil resources in relation to population in the world. Their ratios are clearly above the world average but close to each other: 5.5 for the U.S.S.R. and 6.2 for North America.

Ironically, highly malnourished Latin America has a ratio exceeding 10, which mirrors the lingering effects of the colonial and feudal history of this region. The high ratio is encouraging in one way, since it indicates that drastic adjustment measures could bring this continent back to a reasonable nutritional standard. Such an undertaking, however, would involve a great effort, as close to 50 million people in Latin America are ecologically displaced, tilling land that never should have been broken. They have been forced up the hillsides by plantation crops, the traditional rearing of cattle, and, as in Colombia, even the breeding of race horses.

Finally, Oceania, dominated by Australia and New Zealand, shows

Man's Dominion, 1969-70
(in million PE units)

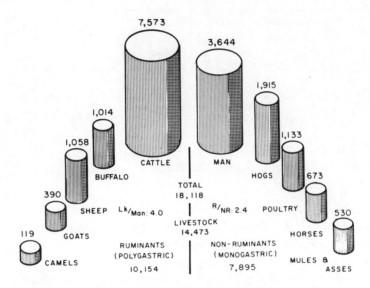

Figure 4: Man's Dominion as to livestock categories for the world.
Cattle are in living mass twice man, and hogs one-half man.

an extremely favorable ratio of above 26. It is important to note, however, that the huge continent of Australia has little more than 12 million people. In land surface it is larger than the United States, but it has less people than the metropolis of Tokyo.

Livestock Categories

The breakdown of man's dominion into livestock categories reveals the prevalence of cattle, in biomass twice that of man (Fig. 4). As protein consumers, hogs are close to half of man. Sheep, poultry, and buffalo each equal one billion PE units. Despite urbanization, horses still account for 673 million PE units.

Vegetarians maintain that if the tremendous living mass of livestock (14.4 billion PE units) were eliminated, the earth could feed that many more people — as if this were the only goal for human strivings. This reasoning overlooks the fact that in the Hungry World a major portion of cattle are actually beasts of burden, not food producers.

It is not merely a coincidence that over 10 billion (10.2) of these population equivalents represent livestock within the ruminant sector. Since ruminants can utilize plant ingredients such as cellulose, hemicellulose, and

Global Biomass* in the Human Sphere (1969-70)
(in billion PE units)

Ruminants (R)		(per cent)	Non-Ruminants (NR)		(per cent)
Cattle	7.57	53.2	Swine	1.92	13.3
Buffalo	1.01	7.1	Poultry	1.13	7.9
Sheep	1.06	7.4	Horses	0.67	4.7
Goats	0.39	2.0	Asses	0.39	2.6
Camels	0.12	0.8	Mules	0.14	1.0
(R)	10.15	70.5	(NR)	4.25	29.5

Total Livestock 14.47 (Ratio R/NR 2.40)

Man   3.65
Grand Total   18.12

* Defined via protein consumption.

others that man's gastric system cannot digest, they considerably broaden the basis for human existence through their low-key competition. They also scan lands man cannot cultivate effectively. Yet non-ruminants may be viewed as competitors to man. Certainly hogs and poultry belong in this category within Western-type agriculture, although in China these two non-ruminants are fed from waste, including sewage. In this respect they provide invaluable recycling and do not compete with man.

Biological Ranking of Countries

When countries are ranked according to total human protein consumption (biological ranking), there is no change in position of the top four countries when listed by number of inhabitants (see table at top of p. 51). But the ratio between livestock and man is less favorable in China than in India. Each of these giants carries a feeding burden exceeding 2 billion PE units. The Soviet Union and the United States come next (1.56 and 1.46 billion respectively).

These data picture the true feeding burden of each country. For example, in order for the United States to feed its 200 million inhabitants, an additional 1.26 billion PE units of livestock (measured in terms of protein intake) have to be accommodated. This is why two-thirds of the tilled acreage in the United States is devoted to the raising of feed crops. This example, while illustrating the true biological dimensions of nutrition, more importantly explodes the simplistic notion that population totals are only a matter of adding numbers of people. In this way the food-and-people relationship is placed in a new and far more accurate illumination.

The four Grand Powers, plus Brazil, each have more than one billion PE units as livestock and poultry. These figures are surprisingly equal, although slightly higher for China. As previously mentioned, however, in

The Human Biosphere in the Four Top Countries
(in billion PE units)

	Man	Livestock	Total	Ratio
China	0.83	1.77	2.60	2.1
India	0.54	1.48	2.02	2.7
U.S.S.R.	0.24	1.32	1.56	5.5
U.S.A.	0.20	1.26	1.46	6.3

China hogs and most poultry do not compete with man but feed on waste and sewage.

Argentina, which ranks 26th on earth in human numbers, moves up in this biological ranking to take the 6th place, and Australia, the 3rd, moves to 8th, and Japan, the 7th, becomes the 20th. There are only a few major countries that are as squeezed as Japan. South Korea, with a ratio of 0.45, is one; Indonesia, with 0.98, is another. The low ratio of livestock to people in one way explains why Japan and these other crowded countries have managed to survive (App. Table 19).

The ratio for New Zealand, in size about equal to Italy or the United Kingdom, is 48.7. The living mass of its sheep, cattle, and other livestock is that many times larger than that of man. Yet, when taking into account the total number in the human biosphere, the differences between the three countries are far less. If the fact that a sizeable portion of the livestock in the United Kingdom and Italy are fed from outside sources is taken into account, the remaining discrepancies even out considerably.

The Human Biosphere in Selected Countries 1969-70
(in million PE units)

	Man	Livestock	Total	Ratio
New Zealand	2.78	135.3	138.1	48.7
Britain (U.K.)	55.5	184.2	239.1	3.3
Italy	53.2	159.2	212.4	3.0
West Germany	60.8	210.0	270.8	3.5
Spain	33.0	99.8	132.7	3.0

Most major European countries show a ratio of around 3 or over, and most are heavily boosted by feed brought in from the United States, tropical Africa, and Argentina, and through the input of fish meal from the ocean. Adjusting the ratio accordingly, Europe's comes close to that of Asia. This interpretation renders new insight into overpopulation.

New Criteria of Overpopulation

Overpopulation has always been poorly defined and can *only* be used in a relative sense. Certainly a country is greatly overpopulated when it relies on large acreages of tilled land or pastures in other lands or continents. It is also overpopulated when it depends on major food contributions from the oceans outside of its fishing grounds. In biologically overdeveloped countries, vanishing forest lands and pastures mirror squeezed conditions, ultimately resulting in declining acreages for food and feed production. More insidious indications of overpopulation are depleted soils, emptied groundwater resources, or declining nutritional standards, especially when forced below the level of minimum needs. These all reflect excessive taxing of capital resources or the inability to sustain minimum requirements.

Still more specific gauges of excessive population pressure are the increasingly devious ways of accommodating added numbers through such measures as substituting plant products for animal foods, and resorting to imbalanced diets with excessive calories and inadequate protein intake. This is often accomplished by increasing the intake of sugar, cassava flour, or cereal grains without a counterbalancing of proteinaceous foods such as beans, nuts, fish, and similar items.

In countries where people suffer protein deficiencies, a decline in the ratio between livestock and man is also noticeable. For example, in Bangladesh this ratio is 1.1 as against 1.7 in Pakistan. The difference in ratio clearly reflects the much greater pressure the human population is exerting in the eastern section. The present ratio in the Nile Valley is 1.52 and on a distinctly downward trend. The island of Java shows a figure of 0.65, incidently identical to that of Japan, as against 1.4 to 1.5 for the so-called Outer Islands of Indonesia. These examples indicate that it is high time the food-and-people relationship be considered in such basic terms.

Chapter 5

The Hunger Gap

No less than 2,500 million of the 3,782 million persons now living on earth (1972) are critically short of most of life's necessities, such as food, water, shelter, clothing and fuel. The lack of water, a Siamese twin of food, is most critical, as no less than 3,000 million, according to a WHO survey, are short of water.

In addition, international agencies have established that at least one billion persons suffer from overt hunger or clear-cut starvation. While some 10 to 20 million die each year from the direct or indirect effects of such causes, these figures are often obscured by acute cases of hunger in regions such as Biafra and Bangladesh which happen to be in the political limelight. Hunger and starvation have always shadowed man, but not until this century have these deprivations affected so many hundreds of millions or such a large proportion of the human race. Food shortages have become chronic and almost global, and in a world now adding more than 75 million people per year, starvation could easily become seriously acute before the year 2000.

The task of feeding the world's growing population will be increasingly difficult. Two-thirds of the world's people live in countries where food is generally in short supply. By 1985, when the population of the globe will approach 5 billion, nearly three-quarters of the world's people will live in food-deficit countries whose populations are increasing more than twice as fast (in per cent) as those of the well-fed world.

What Is Hunger?

A distinction needs to be made between undernutrition and malnutrition. When a person is undernourished, his total daily caloric intake of food does not provide the minimum requirements of energy. Malnutrition is a deficit in specific nutrients, leading to the appearance of visible symptoms. There is, however, no clear line of distinction between these two major categories of hunger.

Hungry Seasons

Seasonal shortages appear in many countries when stored crops run out before the next harvest. Hungry weeks often extend into hungry months as shortages vary from year to year. The most critical deficit areas are encountered in tropical Africa, parts of East and South Asia, and in Latin America. This phenomenon rules harshly and dictates seasonal male migration from African villages to adjacent or distant mining centers and cities, the duration of the stay being correlated to the crop outcome of the year, as pointed out in Chapter 2, p. 23.

Hidden Hunger

Finally, there is "hidden hunger," a term frequently used to describe latent changes or less conspicuous reactions. In some instances only detailed chemical analysis can ascertain the undermined conditions, as in the case of anemias. A more insidious and evasive phenomenon is the "vanishing act" of victims not included in hunger statistics. These include infants who die prior to age three, and people who are so weakened or sick from insufficient food intake that they are bed-ridden.

The Haves and the Have-nots

In sharp contrast to the Hungry World (HW) of 2.5 billion, there is a top group, comprising about 500 million people who live largely in North America, western Europe (including Scandinavia), Australia, New Zealand, and the La Plata region of South America. Even in this top group, some 30 million in the United States receive inadequate food because of low purchasing power, and some 10 million show clear signs of malnutrition. Approximately 700 million people, chiefly in the U.S.S.R., eastern Europe, and Japan, belong to an intermediary group which receives adequate food, but nonetheless sustains itself on a rather monotonous and frugal diet. The Satisfied World (SW) consequently shows a broad amplitude in its nutritive standards and comprises all parts that on the average receive above minimum requirements, i.e. the top group (the well-fed) as well as the intermediary group. Measured in terms of animal protein intake, the United States average is 71* grams (g) per day, 50 percent above the average 48 g/-day of SW, but 5 times the corresponding figure for HW of 10g/day. This gap in dietary terms among the people of the world is sometimes called *the Hunger Gap*, or, when all discrepancies in the standard of living are con-

* the 1971 figure

sidered, *the Haves versus the Have-Nots* (App. Table 20). This discrepancy is persistently widening and at an accelerating rate.

The gap between the "haves" and the "have-nots" will increasingly become the number-one world issue. Most of the "have" countries are continually elevating their favorable positions. The "have-not" countries naturally wish to partake more copiously of the world's goods, but their prospects are not bright. Not only is the gap between the "have" and "have-not" nations widening rather than narrowing, but it probably will continue to expand unless economic development programs are able to outrun population growth. So far this has not been the case, and certainly not in the food issue, despite the scientific and technological advances often designated as the Green Revolution.

During the postwar period a third category has emerged, most accurately described as the "have-mores" or the "super-rich." The broader consequences of the fabulous material gains of this group will be further analyzed in Chapter 9.

The "have-not" nations comprise the overwhelming bulk of mankind. China and India alone encompass close to 1.5 billion people. Of all living human beings almost two out of every five are residents of either of these two countries. Of the seven largest countries, five are in Asia and four are "have-nots." Since they contain a decisive majority of the world's inhabitants, they should hold greater rights and power, recognizing the emotionally surcharged matter of wants and needs. They have much to gain and certainly are entitled to their share of the world's food, feed and energy.

Nutritional Inequities

The populations of Canada, the United States, Europe, Australia, New Zealand, and a few other regions consume 2,800 to 3,300 calories per capita per day, whereas in most of Asia, Africa and Latin America the daily calorie consumption ranges from 1,875 to 2,450.

Total protein intake, in grams per head per day, ranges from 106 in New Zealand and 96 in the United States to 59 in West Africa, and around 50 in Monsoon Asia, Southwest Asia and 68 in Latin America. In terms of animal proteins the differences are even sharper. North America has an intake nine times that of Monsoon Asia. The major portions of the food-scarce regions of the world suffer primarily from a shortage of protein, resulting in deficiencies.

Protein malnutrition as evidenced in kwashiorkor and marasmus is most prevalent in some Caribbean countries, like Martinique and Haiti, and in the humid tropical parts of West Africa and Indonesia (in particular Java). On the whole these areas show some of the lowest levels of protein intake in the present world. Those sectors of the population with low purchasing power, both in rural and urban areas, are in a similar way afflicted in most Latin American countries, involving many with seemingly acceptable average figures. Good such examples are Mexico, Brazil, Venezuela, Jamaica, Puerto Rico and Trinidad — see further p. 56-57.

In most developing countries, the inadequacies are not only in the quantity of food, but also in its quality — inadequacies which lead to malnutrition as well as undernutrition. The diets of these people are generally low in calories and imbalanced in other nutrients, because they consist mainly of cereals and starchy foods. The lack of variety in the diet and particularly the shortage of protective foods such as milk, eggs, fish, and meat contribute to inadequate intake of vitamins, minerals and high-quality protein. These deficiencies in turn lead to the incidence of specific diseases which are particularly prevalent in Middle America, Africa, and part of Asia. Beri-beri persists as a serious illness in the rice-eating areas of Asia, while other diseases, such as anemia, avitaminosis A, goiter, rickets, and pellagra, are more generally distributed throughout the developing countries.

Efforts to improve the world's food supply have concentrated on quantity — the caloric value of food output. Yet, inhabitants of many deficit areas suffer from malnutrition resulting from a diet lacking in protein. Although the world produces an adequate amount of protein-rich food to fill overt deficiencies, there is not enough to fill the minimum requirements of all. Most high-quality protein in the form of milk, meat, and eggs is consumed as well as produced in the developed countries, where, in contrast to less-developed countries, the acreage for raising feed crops and the means for massive purchases of feeding stuffs are available. Disproportionate amounts of protein from feedgrains, palm kernels, oilseeds, and fish meal are channelled into this animal production of the well-to-do, thus inflicting major conversion losses to the human household of precious protein.

The need for protein varies from one section of the population to another. Children and pregnant women require more protein than others, but in the underdeveloped countries they are less likely to consume any more than the average amount. This means that protein deficiency may well exist in a country which on a nationwide basis seems to produce adequate supplies.

There is a broad intermediary zone between dietary deficiency and adequacy. Long before dietary deficits result in visible disturbances, such as stunted growth or skin or bone disruption, eye defects, or mental retardation, many other defined bodily functions and metabolic processes are clearly impaired. For example, susceptibility to diseases and to parasites is such an early insidious effect.

Masking Statistics

The most common mistake in judging nutritional shortages is to concentrate on averages which all too often mask ugly realities. Even in countries where average food consumption levels appear to be adequate, there are major disparities in intake, and large portions of the population are often underfed. In hungry countries discrepancies as a rule are even greater. For example, Mexico shows acceptable averages — just on the borderline — yet there are two Mexicos. Nearly 60 per cent of Mexico's 54 millions have not been the beneficiaries of the recent economic miracle and even show a deterioration in nutritional terms. The Italian intake of animal protein is one-third that of the United States, but many eat very extravagantly. For each Italian who eats three times the national average, there are as many receiving almost as little as a person in India. The fallacy of these averages is one of the least understood or heeded aspects of the food-and-people issue. Purchasing power is the chief factor playing on this scene — and growing numbers is the most destructive undermining force.

As pointed out previously, calorie-rich plant products dominate in daily food of HW. Regions exclusively depending on tubers, like sweet potato, taro, and cassava, are most critical as beans provide no adequate protein supplementation. The only recourse is animal protein, fish in most instances being the singular alternative available.

If all the food in the world were equally distributed and each human being received identical quantities, we would all be malnourished. If the entire world's food supply were parcelled out at the U.S. dietary level, it would feed only about one-third of the human race. The world as a global household knows of no surpluses, merely enormous deficits. Yet in the well-fed nations there is a great deal of nonsensical talk about abundance and self-sufficiency.

Production Gap

The Hunger Gap needs to be more clearly focused in areas other than nutrition. The advanced industrial countries are generally in the rich category, while the developing countries are in the poor. The discrepancy between the two categories can be measured by the output and consumption, not only of industrial goods, but also of agricultural produce. Of the global wheat output in 1969-70 (average), totaling 314 million metric tons, more than two-thirds (208 million) was produced by advanced countries (U.S.S.R., Europe, U.S. and Canada). Of the total world output of corn (maize) for the same period, amounting to 266 million metric tons, 47 per cent (124 million) was produced by the United States alone.

The discrepancy is still greater when measuring animal production. For instance, the SW, comprising a little above one-fourth of the world in human numbers, accounts for two-thirds to four-fifths of the global production of milk, meat and eggs (App. Table 14).

Another imbalance exists in the production and distribution of fertilizer. As previously mentioned (see Chapter 3, p. 42), until the 1960's less than one-eighth of the world's commercial fertilizers reached developing

Gains in Fertilizer Use SW — HW
(in million metric tons)

	SW	HW	Total
Total NPK			
1955-57 to 1970-71	33.3	11.6	44.9
Per cent	161	464	194
N-fertilizers			
1955-57 to 1970-71	16.6	7.7	24.3
Per cent	345	637	405

countries, where they were largely used for plantation crops to be exported. Once again percentages play a distorting trick. From 1955 to 1971, the HW, with two-thirds of the world's peoples, shows a gain in terms of tonnage which is one-third of that in the SW, yet the percentage jump is three times greater! Similar trends apply to nitrogen fertilizers.

The poverty of the HW prevents many necessary investments in agriculture. Because of yield constraints, all inputs are far more costly than in the SW. It should also be noted that most Western technology is less suited for application in the warm latitudes of the HW. The developed world tends to be far too wasteful with raw materials, water, and energy to allow copying on a global scale. Furthermore, it is geared towards reducing man-hours, the only true surplus of the HW. Studies by Western experts have convincingly proven that both the Chinese and Indian farmers, within the framework of their operating conditions and the resources available to them, are frequently far more efficient than the Western farmer. The same is true of several other countries in the HW. The overwhelming number of farmers in developing countries are tied to soils with considerably less productive potential than the majority of those farms abandoned as non-competitive in the West. Remember, too, many farmers in the developing world are handicapped by undernourishment and ensuing diseases.

In developing countries where agriculture is generally of great importance to the economy, and where the need for additional food supplies is urgent, farmers have far less leeway in utilizing modern farming, and animal husbandry techniques (see Chapter 3). On the other hand, in most industrialized countries agriculture tends to be a minor sector of the economy. Such countries seem to have less difficulty feeding themselves. Although they do not necessarily produce substantially more food relative to population than do many less-developed ones, they use their purchasing power to supplement food production on a major scale (see Chapter 6). Obviously, few developing countries generate enough foreign exchange to pay for food imports. As a result the world food market is often characterized by increasing surpluses and falling producer prices in developed countries, while scarcity of food causes high consumer prices in less-developed countries.

There appears to be a renewed emphasis on improving agricultural conditions in some of the less-developed countries themselves. More investment funds are currently being allocated to the agricultural sector of the economy after more than a decade in which industrial investments overshadowed those in other sectors. This revised strategy has resulted in the Green Revolution, but its success hinges upon the resource basis and above all on population control.

As the Hunger Gap Widens . . .

The widening hunger gap is an ominous feature of our days and one which poses the greatest challenge mankind has ever faced, overshadowing atom bombs, continental missiles, microbial toxins and nerve gases. The relentless greed of the "haves" and the "have-mores" is not only highly calamitous but indicates perverted goals in a world where parsimony, moderation, and responsibility should be our guides.

Chapter 6

The Trade Illusion

In global terms world trade can be best described on the basis of the net outflow and net influx to each continent (App. Table 22).* North America stands out as the globe's prime provider of food and feed, with the United States accounting for three-fourths and Canada for one-fourth of its contribution to the world household. South America comes second with Argentina (meat, grain and oilseeds) and Brazil (coffee, meat, and other products) in the lead. Africa is a close third, primarily through peanuts, palm kernels, and other oilseeds. Fourth rank is held by Australia and New Zealand. It is worth noting that the world's grasslands (the prairies, the pampas, the llanos, the grasslands of Africa and Australia) are a keystone in this structure, a pattern created by the grand European drive and little modified by subsequent developments.

One major change from the postwar world is that Asia has switched from a net provider to a net importer. In one way this turnabout may be looked upon as a late acknowledgment of the needs of this huge continent, as Asia is now attaining 2 billion and is rapidly moving towards holding in year 2000 as many people as the globe today. Closer scrutiny reveals, however, that the decisive factor in this switch has primarily been the disproportionate demands of the 106 million Japanese, which is further analyzed below.

Fewer Net-Exporters

In terms of individual countries the last 25 years have seen the number of net exporters dwindle, or their deliveries shrink. Only the United States and Canada remain major net providers to the world household. Argentina, Australia, and New Zealand belong here but are far smaller, with

* In terms of *trade acreage* = tilled land required to raise the netwise import or export.

the first two mentioned being less dependable as to volume. Others only have marginal significance. Several countries like Denmark, the Netherlands, France, and a few others figure prominently as exporters but make no net contribution as their deliveries are balanced out by correspondingly larger imports of food and feed from outside. France, for instance, is importing more than half of the fat its people consume.

Several countries have continued to export particular commodities, but under the pressure of growing numbers many have been forced to a countervailing importation of essential food; among examples are Egypt (cotton versus grains) and Cuba (sugar versus grains). Some have been forced to curtail consumption; for instance, Argentina, for which beef is almost a national symbol, has been forced into meatless days — recently expanded to meatless weeks.

Chief Recipient

The major recipient of the global deliveries of food and feed is Europe, in particular its western countries, joined, however, by the eastern section in the 1960's. The pattern established by the Europeans in the Big Grab (see Chapter 1) has been sustained. Even when the worldwide surge toward national independence after World War II (1945-50), which involved more than one and a half billion people, marked the political end to the grand Western era, Western man retained his economic dominance, especially in trade and marketing.

Most notable is the fact that the United Kingdom and West Germany each far surpass India as world recipients of food and feed (for cereals, see App. Table 24). Since 1940 Asia has switched from a net-exporting to a net-importing continent, often interpreted as a result of its increase in numbers. While this is true to a minor degree, the major factor is the growing affluence of Japan, which accounts for a disproportionate share of this importation. With its 106 million people Japan is receiving more imports than China and India combined, although these latter two countries total 1,370 million people. Except for Japan and parts of southwest Asia, the undernourished millions of Asia get very little from outside their own continent. What would world trade look like if they were to receive even a fraction of what well-fed Europe is getting? For all practical purposes Asia is highly self-contained, with Japan the unique and glaring exception.

The U.S.S.R. is a special case, needing some explanation. In czarist days Russia was a grain-selling nation. Ukraine, then called Scythia, was one of the grain baskets of the Roman Empire. Through the centuries it remained a grain provider and constituted the back-up of Europe before the North American prairie started to take over that position in the 19th century. After the 1850's, deforestation coupled with grave soil erosion reduced

Ukraine's grain-producing capabilities. The drought vagaries of the Ukrainian climate soon made this source of grain less dependable, and the Soviet Union was forced to create new grain baskets further east. As a result the average size of its grain crop (in wheat twice that of the United States) has firmly maintained the U.S.S.R. as a net exporter, although the drought spell of 1964-66 made the U.S.S.R. a net importer for the first time. In 1972 the U.S.S.R. had to import again, this time because of the late arrival of summer and poor harvesting conditions. The postwar swing to animal products, which pushed back the traditional bread and potato diet, is a major factor in the size of the purchases in this recent shortage crisis.

For almost four centuries the Caribbean was a net exporting region through sugar but became increasingly dependent on the purchase of grain, now top-ranking per capita. We frequently hoist the flag of the world's hungry, but facts speak another language. Denmark, Israel, and the Netherlands are the world's leading importers of plant protein (Fig. 5). The 5 million Danes carry the world record as protein importers, primarily for livestock feed; they average 214 lbs. per person a year. In the mid 1960's the Netherlands imported more non-fat milk solids (to raise veal) than the entire Hungry World (HW) received. Furthermore, this tiny country imports 17.5 lbs (1969-70) of protein per person a year in the form of fish meal, another world record. This amount contains seven times more protein than from the direct intake of fish and is equivalent to the milk intake per person in this dairy country. Yet the absurd notion exists that the Netherlands, a net-importing country, could constitute a model for the HW.

Import of Plant Protein, 1967-68
(in kilograms per capita)

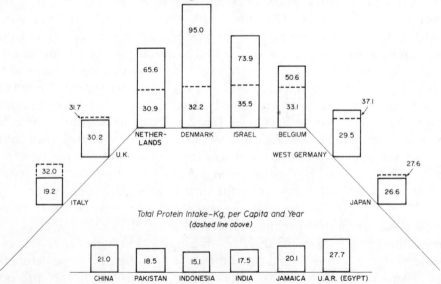

Total Protein Intake–Kg. per Capita and Year
(dashed line above)

Figure 5: Purchases of plant protein through World Market on a per capita basis (upper section). Compare with total intake of protein in selected countries (lower section), and in each purchasing nation (indicated by dotted line).

The U.S. — A Big Buyer

In recent years the United States has become top-ranking in the world market as a buyer of beef, even surpassing the United Kingdom (App. Table 23). The United States procures its beef not only from Australia and New Zealand, but from several countries of Central and South America such as Mexico, Brazil and Costa Rica, all of which happen to be critically short of both meat and protein.

A significant feature of the postwar world is the influx of foods and food products from the entire world into the United States, placing products from all corners of the globe within easy reach. Walking through a modern American supermarket is like taking a world tour: bananas from Ecuador, Costa Rica, and other Latin American countries, coffee from Brazil and Colombia, sardines from Southwest Africa, pineapples from Taiwan and the Philippines, fish dumplings from Norway, pickled herring from Sweden, mandarines (tangerines) from Japan, hams from Poland, Denmark, the Netherlands and Canada, corned beef from Argentina and Brazil, frozen shrimp from more than 50 countries, cheeses from Italy, France and Scandinavia, kangaroo soup from Australia, and so on.

This exuberant abundance has led most Americans to believe in the long-standing Western notion, shared by western Europe, that the world constitutes an overflowing cornucopia. In particular the tropics have been regarded as a rich fountain from which comes a seemingly endless stream of "goodies" such as bananas, coffee, cacao, sugar, tropical fruits, oilseeds, and oilseed cakes. Yet the image is fading fast, heralding completely new patterns in both world economy and world trade. The countries of the HW desperately need the lands rendering these riches in order to feed themselves. So far we have exhibited little awareness of what is happening, yet the unmistakable signs are there — all the elements of a new world order. An American historian once remarked that the Western world has a queer affinity for "fighting history rather than adjusting to it."

Global Aspects of Trade

International trade in agricultural products has rarely exceeded one-tenth of total production. Only for a few commodities is it higher (App. Table 25). The major share of this exchange of foods and feeds moves between well-satisfied and rich countries. Grain, potatoes, beans, sugar, oilseeds, and fruit, in that order, are the leaders in volume. As a consequence world trade removes little of the inequities of the globe. Instead its overall effect on the net flow is the reverse. Absurdly enough, with the exception of food grain, the net exchange between the HW and the SW definitely favors the well-fed world. Even the tremendous grain deliveries through aid programs have done little to bridge the hunger gap, and no serious effort has ever been made to incorporate these deliveries into any kind of normal trade. It is feed grains that currently dominate the international grain trade, largely moving from North America to Europe (App. Table 26).

Prior to World War II food grains also moved from the HW to the SW, a pattern which still remains dominant in the trade of oilseeds, peanuts, palm kernels, copra, oilseed cake and meal. Through oilseeds, oilseed products, and fish meal, the Western world is currently acquiring from the HW one million metric tons more protein than is delivered to the HW through grains. In other words, the Western world is exchanging approximately 3 million metric tons of cereal protein for 4 million metric tons of other proteins which are all superior in a nutritive respect. This flow from the HW is depriving millions in tropical Africa, Latin America, and Asia of their major deficit commodity. The SW is thus taking no small amount of protein from the world's scarce supplies. In addition, close to half of the ocean catches are ear-marked to provide feed protein and food fat to the SW — catches that largely originate in the waters of the two most protein-deficient continents of South America (Peru and Chile) and Africa (South and Southwest, and Angola). Europe alone is currently importing around 1.7 million tons of fish meal protein annually.

The massive European net importation of plant protein (in 1968-69 on the average of 10 million metric tons) makes it possible for that continent to uphold a high nutritive standard, gauged in terms of animal protein intake. The influx of oilseeds, and oilseed cake and meal, is one of the keys to Europe's high animal production. Soybeans, imported chiefly from the United States, and fish meal are the other two major factors in the almost miraculous postwar expansion in animal production of eastern and western Europe. This transoceanic flow accounts for two-fifths of the gain (Compare App. Tables 27, 28, 29).

North American milk production is firmly based on American soybeans, and soybeans rank next to oilseed cakes as a source of external protein for Europe. In fact, the dairy production and margarine manufacture of the entire Western world is closely tied to soybeans. Less than 3 per cent of the soybeans exported from the United States currently feed the hungry. We have hardly begun to mobilize this invaluable resource in the Great Battle for Human Survival. Only one-tenth of the soybeans utilized domestically in the United States enter into direct human consumption. On the other hand, in China, Japan, and Korea, the soybean is a key human food. With their excessive population numbers, these countries cannot afford anything else. Early in their history they were forced to take this road.

Prior to World War II India used to be a leading exporter of peanuts, thus contributing to the feeding of the United Kingdom and its cattle. The pattern changed during and after the war. In recent years, however, there has been a partial reversal in this trend and India once again has become the world's leading exporter of peanut cake and meal, accounting for 42 per cent of the total world trade and even surpassing tropical Africa's total sale of this commodity (App. Table 30). India's deliveries go primarily to the United Kingdom, France, West Germany, and Czechoslovakia.

Hungry World Gets a Trickle

The ironical outcome of world trade is that two-thirds of the world's agricultural production is consumed or utilized by less than one-third of the world's people. The same wide discrepancy applies to the oceans with only one-fourth of the ocean catches reaching consumers in the poor world.

This overall picture may be somewhat surprising in light of the large postwar relief deliveries of food to India, Pakistan, and China. Through Public Law 480 major quantities of grain have reached the needy world from the United States. In the mid-1960's the product of each fifth wheat acre in the United States was earmarked for shipment to India. Many other countries (Canada, Australia, France) also made significant contributions. Nonetheless, these massive deliveries of grain hardly amounted to more than a few per cent of the consumption in the importing countries, providing mainly the recipient port cities and coastal regions. The same applies to the multi-million-ton grain shipments to China from Canada and Australia.

Hungry World Supplies Satisfied World

Despite these deliveries from the granaries of the affluent, the HW is still earmarking large portions of its scanty soil resources as well as toiling hard to provide food and feed to the SW, which in turn depends on the HW through the import of cash crops. Besides oilseed crops, much good soil in Latin America, tropical Africa and parts of Asia produces sugar, coffee, cacao, tea, bananas, and cotton which are sold largely to the SW. Until the recent Green Revolution, irrigation and fertilizers were reserved almost exclusively for the soils of these export crops. An overwhelming number of farmers are still forced to eke out an existence, squeezing out food for subsistence and domestic markets from soils which should be classified marginal in comparison to those utilized for cash crops. Many of these soils are so deficient and lacking in water that they should never have been cultivated; they are also frequently located on hillsides or steep gradients. In this respect close to 50 million people in Latin America can be classified as ecologically displaced persons. They desperately need to be moved to acceptable lands before their topsoil is forever gone. Ironically, in North America and parts of Europe marginal lands which frequently carry soils with far better productive potentials in terms of basic fertility and availability of water are being abandoned.

The economic returns of the cash crop sales are becoming increasingly fictitious as the price of raw materials on the world market declines, while the price of needed capital goods climbs. Since 1952 the HW has increased the volume of its agricultural exportation by more than one-third with a net gain in cash income of only 4 per cent. Paradoxically, the poor countries have to pay more and more in product volume for each purchased manufactured import. Furthermore, due to the population pressure and food shortage, a growing percentage of the earnings goes into buying food, often quite costly compared to the inadequate economic gains. On the Ivory Coast imported protein in the shape of canned meat, milk and fish costs about 11 times more than the exported protein in the shape of peanuts and oilseed cakes.

A Basic Fallacy

The conventional rationale for this trade has been the acquisition of foreign currency, a principle which has turned out to be largely fallacious. The foreign currencies only erratically become available for rational use. Taxation efficiency, among other things, is wholly inadequate in most of these countries. The dropping world market prices, usually fixed by the SW, have drastically cut net gains. A 5 per cent drop in prices of world commodities almost nullifies all capital contributions through foreign aid. This phenomenon may also be formulated in the following way: declining net income due to increasingly less favorable terms of trade for raw materials versus industrial products.

The traditional concept of raw material countries as opposed to industrialized countries — largely a remnant of 19th century thinking — is also becoming an anachronism in the food sector. One major driving force is obviously the global availability or universality of technical knowledge. This is no longer the exclusive domain of the Western world or any individual country, however advanced it may be. Future generations, therefore, are not likely to experience the thrill of holding an orange, a banana, or even a handful of coffee beans, as the orange skins, the banana peel and the coffee grounds are far too valuable to the producing country as animal feed. Future economists and historians will marvel that in 1970, 70 per cent of the world's registered fleet of refrigerated ships were completely tied up carrying bananas from the tropics to North America and western Europe (App. Table 31). Half of the carried weight is stock and peel, which currently end up in our garbage cans. Despite modern facilities in delivery and receiving ports and tremendous fleets of refrigerated trucks and railroad cars, the losses of bananas are estimated to exceed one-tenth. The elements of a new order, however, are emerging with profound repercussions. Several plants are manufacturing less-perishable items such as banana flakes, flour and chips, and are already providing the world market with a new array of foods, thus contributing to a less-wasteful economy. The same applies to the new industrial plants in Brazil and other tropical coffee-growing countries which are manufacturing soluble coffee and coffee concentrates.

The Illusion of Self-Sufficiency

The term self-sufficiency and the corresponding notion that a country produces most of what it eats from its own soil is grossly misleading in several ways. Few concepts contribute more to a blurred understanding of the relationship between food and population (App. Table 32). Japan is commonly referred to as a country with 80 per cent self-sufficiency. Yet, in most commodities used as food and feed, the reliance on trade is unbelievably great.

Japan — Import in Percentage of Domestic Production

Production in Million Metric Tons			Import in Per Cent of Total Use (A)	
1964-66	1969-70		1964-66	1969-70
0.07	0.94	Corn	98	99
1.18	0.62	Wheat	76	80
1.18	0.69	Barley	31	38
16.34	17.2	Rice	6.5	3.0
0.22	0.14	Soybeans	87.5	93
0.94	0.43	Sugar	83	83
0.79	0.74	Meat	35	39
19.0	18.8	Cereals	35	41

The Netherlands is portrayed as a country flowing with milk and honey. It has always been considered a significant exporter of eggs, bacon, cheese, oilseed cake, and similar items. Nonetheless, the Netherlands has for centuries been a net-importing country, depending on a constant influx of grain, oilseed, oilseed cake, and similar items. By the early 18th century additional grain was being procured from the Baltic countries, later from the Ukraine, and ultimately from the North American prairie.

The degree of self-sufficiency is mostly measured in simplified economic terms. As soon as a country is capable of raising a crop to a volume which can meet the market needs as reflected in the purchasing power of the consumer, it is categorized as self-sufficient in that commodity. On that basis South Africa and Pakistan, among others, have reported "surpluses" to international agencies, despite extensive unmet needs. This brings up still another trap in the use of this term. Any country, even a malnourished one, can easily — chiefly because of highly defective agricultural planning — build up unsalable amounts of almost any crop. Such surpluses are basically artificial and illusionary. Only when the totality of the major crops, vital as food or feed, is adequate, is the concept of self-sufficiency a reality. Obviously this concept needs redefining. A country is only self-sufficient when the net trade of agricultural food products is in positive balance and no malnutrition due to shortage of food prevails.

India was until quite recently (spring, 1973) under the euphoria of the Green Revolution, claiming self-sufficiency in total grains, which is certainly a step forward compared to earlier loose talk about self-sufficiency in wheat and rice respectively. Yet the image is critically eclipsed. This alleged grain sufficiency was reached by a critical reduction in the bean acreages, crucial to balancing out the cereals in terms of protein adequacy (see Chapter 3). The truth of the matter is that India needs more than a doubling of its crop production to satisfy the minimal needs of its present population. During 1972-73 the harsh realities of the capricious monsoon affected major parts of India, in the Northeast through drought and in the Southwest through floods, resulting in the build-up of critical grain shortages.

In principle the contributions from the oceans in the form of proteins and fats should be recognized. When this is done, almost no country on earth remains in the favorable position of feeding from its own resources. If oceanic dependence is not taken into account, the number of net-exporting countries has been critically reduced since 1900. Only five countries remain as significant contributors to the world household (the United States, Canada, Argentina, Australia, and New Zealand). Some 15 countries are still upholding a facade as net exporters, but at the expense of the nutritive well-being of their citizens, or at the expense of the soils, which are undergoing an insidious degradation through erosion, mineral depletion and dessication. It is about time the relationship between food and population were analyzed from these vantage points.

The Per-Capita Upset

The food-and-people relationship in trade is rarely ever analyzed on a per capita basis (Fig. 6). Generally volume and values, in themselves important figures to most discussions and analyses, are not sufficient for the purposes of relating food to people, as they distort the true significance of food and feed transfer between countries. The following examples underline the need for another area of emphasis.

When global wheat trade is analyzed on the basis of such per capita data, Cuba and Israel emerge as the world's top-ranking importers (App. Table 26). On the whole the Caribbean stands out as a cardinal recipient of this key grain, although competing with several European countries: the Netherlands, Norway, and the United Kingdom in the west, Czechoslovakia and East Germany in the east. China and India move to the bottom of the import list. Even when taking into account that alternative grains (rice and millets) cover part of the intake of these two countries, their minor

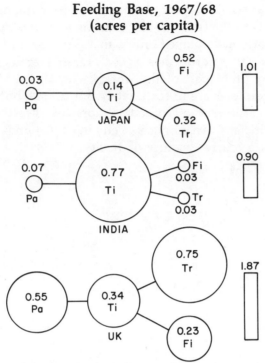

Feeding Base, 1967/68
(acres per capita)

Figure 6:   Feeding Base of Japan, India, and the
United Kingdom in acres per capita. Ti = Tilled
land; Fi = Fish acreage; Tr = Trade acreage; Pa =
Pastures. All of these components are added
together in the total feeding base (bars to the right).
Note the lack of correlation between these data and
that of acreages of tilled land.

dependence on trade makes this transfer of wheat around the globe almost
irrelevant to their hundreds of millions. Yet they are in the top in total tonnage of imports, with the United Kingdom their chief contender.

The rice picture is also upset by similar data and emerges in a new
light. The parade of importers is led by the urban centers of Hong Kong,
Singapore, and others, followed by South Vietnam, the greatest importer in
total volume. As pointed out earlier only a small fraction of the world's rice
production ever enters world trade.

Distorting the Truth

In the *OECD* Recommendations on Food Problems of Less Developed Countries* (1967) the following priceless statements are encountered:

"— recognizing that the developed countries have been increasingly
supplementing the food supply of the developing countries" — The reverse
assertion would better fit the facts.

* Organization for Economic Cooperation and Development

"—noting that reliance cannot be placed on food imports alone (!) to provide a solution (!) to the food problems in the less developed regions of the world."* —Imports have played only a marginal role in the HW. Contrast this with the fact that Europe has placed a far greater degree of reliance on imports than any other part of the world.

These two examples are unfortunately not unique but rather reflect the thinking and attitudes of broad sectors of Western scientists, economists, and politicians. An ethnocentricity in education is distorting the truth and giving us a blurred picture of reality.

*Interjection signs inserted by author.

Chapter 7

The Urban Trap

A highly distressing feature of our immediate future is the accelerated urbanization of the world. During the past 100 years the world's population has almost tripled (from 1,340 million in 1870, to 3,782 million in 1972), but the proportion that lives in cities has increased sevenfold. Mushrooming urban growth has produced the slums and shanty towns in which one-third of today's city-dwellers are living under conditions inimical to health. The urban calamities around the globe are reiterated almost daily in news media: menacing air and water pollution, pall-shrouding smog, water restrictions, traffic congestion, and human misery in general. The list is almost endless. Vice, criminality, malnutrition, and mental illness are only part of the social disturbances that inevitably trail urbanization.

This analysis will not elaborate on man's obvious shortcomings in adequately providing for the human family when transferring operations from rural expanses to contained urban settings. Rather it will probe the functionality of the urban principle by studying it from vantage points other than the traditional ones. This endeavor is an attempt to dispel some of the verbal mist presently surrounding both the concept and phenomenon of urbanization. Only by focusing attention on the key issues of food and population does it become obvious how much we are resorting to escapism.

Few sociologists and historians have grasped the true nature or global magnitude of the urban crisis. Unfortunately, man is perpetuating false notions with his words and is falling victim to a large-scale deception. The massive migrations into cities, paralleling the rising tide in human numbers, are simply viewed as a kind of magical, irresistible force, at times even termed progressive. As so often happens, hidden behind the astounding statistical data is the suffering of millions, which Western man has completely obliterated from his conscious awareness. All the crisis phenomena can be lumped together under the simple heading, *urbanization*. We need to be awakened to the harsh fact that these matters no longer can be relegated to providence or prayer. Far less can they be allowed to be the playgrounds for technocratic toying. Not only engineers but all of mankind must jointly prepare to accommodate vastly growing numbers in cities.

The Malignancy of Urban Growth

At the beginning of the 19th century, only 2 per cent of the world population lived in cities, and not more than 50 cities had populations exceeding 100,000. Today the shanty towns on the fringes of cities alone hold 12 per cent of the earth's people. By the end of the present century, when global population is expected to exceed 7,000 million, six people out of ten are expected to live in cities. Few seem to realize that we are in the midst of what is the most gigantic and most dramatic migration in human history. This huge flow is expected to reach almost 600 million within the 1970's, swelling the numbers of city inhabitants to no less than 1.9 billion by 1980. The urbanized masses will reach about 3 billion by 1990 and 4 billion by year 2000, or more than the entire world population of today.

Almost with pride it is pointed out that these new conglomerates will not be pitifully small, like present-day New York or Tokyo, but will house several tens of millions (São Paulo, 70 million; Calcutta, 60 million). By 1980 each of 18 cities in Latin America is anticipated to be above the million mark. Calcutta, with a population density twice that of Chicago and with 70 per cent of its families living in single rooms and uncounted thousands on the pavements, by 1980 may reach the 15-million mark. Even in tropical Africa, where large-scale urbanization still lies in the future, many countries show half the number of their citizens living in a single metropolitan area. All of these cities appear to be hastening to the million mark before even 5 per cent of their people are engaged in industry.

The gigantic scale of this migration is in itself enough to suggest that urbanization is running the obvious risk of collapsing both in the Hungry and the Satisfied World. Urban expansion has become pathological and threatens to overlay and stunt the healthiest elements of expansion.

The Prime Crisis Area

Since development in general is coupled with urbanization, it is not surprising that in 1920 the developed regions were far ahead in numbers of town-dwellers: 185 million people in towns of over 20,000, with 80 million of those in big cities. For less-developed countries, the figures were then 68 million in towns and only 16 million in big cities.

During the next 40 years the urban citizens of the developing world were hurrying to catch up in numbers and by 1960 had reached 319 million, with 139 million in big cities. In other words, they had multiplied nearly *five times*, while developed urban populations had only a little more than doubled. The big-city figure, that is, the figure for vast mother cities where the great concentrations of slums and shanty towns are to be found, is even more startling. Big cities grew about two and a half times in the developed world, but in the developing regions this growth was more than eightfold.

The Urban Tide 1920-1980
(Million people in cities of more than 20,000)

Year	HW	SW	Total World
1920	68	185	349
1960	319	433	1,100
1970	630	700	1,330
1980*	1,030	895	1,925

Growth

Time Period			
1920-60	251	248	499
1960-70	311	267	578
1970-80*	400	195	595

*Projected

What makes this current urban build-up almost cataclysmic in its implications is the fact that no less than 400 million of these migrants belong in the HW whose cities will add more people within this decade than now live in all of the rural regions of the SW. In most instances a massive, multimillion slum proletariat will result. Yet this development will not avert a further growth of the rural proletariat. In other words, within *one brief decade* the cities of the developing world will be expected to take care of more than half the number of people which now are accommodated in all the cities of the developed world — the equivalent of two United States' in human numbers. In addition, during the same decade the developing world must supply an amount of housing, administration buildings, schools, hospitals, transport, and employment facilities equivalent to what has been built in all of the cities in the developed world over centuries of growth. So far the dimensions of this herculean undertaking are very poorly perceived.

The urbanization of the HW is a far more sinister and complex phenomenon than we normally acknowledge. The pressure on the countryside is reaching the boiling point. Farms have been cut up into "miniplots" of one to two acres for the feeding of a family, and shanty towns, garbage dumps and gravel pits are becoming the domiciles of millions. In several instances this influx has already reached unmanageable proportions, especially in some cities of Latin America and Asia.

Latin America

The populations of Latin America are growing at an average of 2.8 per cent annually, or by nearly 8.5 million persons a year. Cities in Brazil, Venezuela, Argentina and other countries are growing at phenomenal rates as a result of the accelerated movement of people from the rural areas. There is a swelling internal movement from the backlands into a few big cities. As a result most of these have grown much faster than the water, light, housing, or even food facilities could be expanded.

Many of these cities have an ultra-modern appearance; their architects lead the world in creating new forms. The inhabitants also are rapidly abandoning their traditional ways of living. Yet the most characteristic features are still the swelling shanty towns,* and the expanding misery of the growing cadres of squatters. They are the garbage can raiders, ragpickers, tin-can collectors, bottle gatherers, and wastepaper bundlers, who can always glean something from dumping places to sell to junkyards. Far too many in the South American slums are the working ants trying to salvage something from the refuse of their more fortunate brothers. Like human buzzards they find their daily food in garbage cans.

Each year 75,000 Peruvians move into Lima, the capital, with most ending in slum areas, "chorillos." In 1955 Lima had one million inhabitants, one-tenth of whom lived in slums, but in 1968 there were 2.1 million, with one-fifth in slums. Now (1972) there are 2.8 million, with half in rejected housing and one-third in slums. The influx has accelerated, and the slum expansions have become more brutal.

Between 1960 and 1975 the cities of Latin America are expected to grow by 100 million! The present urban growth rate is 5 to 6 per cent annually, which means that they are doubling in size within less than 15 years. In cities of about 100,000 no less than two-thirds of the inhabitants live in slums. In the big metropoli this figure is around one-third. These shanty towns often perch dangerously on steep hills or stand on stilts in swampy lowlands, since such land areas are the only ones available and within reach for squatting. This is certainly a dismal picture for a rich continent, but one which has been overtaken or overrun by too many people. Despite the fact that the wheels are rolling full speed, the task is oversized.

The Wretchedness of Urban Blight

Journalists endlessly depict the tragedy of the homeless in cities like Djakarta, Calcutta (more than a million) and numerous others, describing how not only the sidewalks but also the streets are crowded at night by sleeping people. For example, in Bogota, Colombia, some 50,000 to 70,000 children bundle up in the streets each night.

* Vernacular for shanty towns or slum areas: barriadas (Peru), chorillos (Lima, Peru), bidonvilles (Paris, France), bustees (India), colonias proletarias (Mexico), gecekondu (Turkey), gourbivilles (Tunisia), ranchos (Venezuela), favelas (Rio de Janeiro, Brazil).

The plight and blight of large cities is most conspicuous in housing. In the Western world we consider our housing shortage as staggering. Yet our hardship is mild compared to that of the less-affluent world. Most Latin American nations are faced with excruciating housing shortages. Figures and data abound, but neither action nor planning is keeping pace. The continent of South America needs a sixfold increase in its housing construction. One-fourth of Manila's population, some 800,000 persons in 130,000 families, live under subhuman conditions in unbelievable slums. Djakarta, the capital of Indonesia, is a crowded city of around 6 million people, three-quarters of whom live in inadequate housing or no housing at all. Djakarta has received most of the overflow from the villages of Java and has grown by about 6 per cent a year. In anticipation of a natural-growth population close to 8 million in 1985, the city in 1971 was closed to new migrants unless they had jobs or homes.

Millions who are dumped in cities scrounge for food in the garbage dumps. Water facilities are either lacking or wholly inadequate. Natural waters, when available, are the only recourse and serve for laundry, bathing, defecating, and garbage disposal — and worst of all, also for drinking. No wonder schools and hospitals can take care of only a portion of what is needed. In Djakarta there is just one hospital bed for every 1,250 persons. Similar or worse figures are quoted from many big cities in the developing world. By contrast, in Japan there is one bed for every 90 persons.

Targets are established in development programs for the construction of schools, clinics, roads, and water supplies, but food and food-marketing facilities are notoriously missing. Mysterious automatic forces are believed to handle these matters. When considered, it is only those with an adequate purchasing power that count. Effective demand rules supremely, blind to the garbage raiders, the hungry, starving, and malnourished.

In the late 20th century the transmissions belt into the cities have been persistently pouring in new migrant multitudes, not into a potentially viable order but into a wilderness, where opportunities are shrinking and the millions are piling on top of one another. The farms do not feed them, nor do the industries employ them. The root of much of the developing world's trouble lies in this distorted, bloated, and unmanageable urban sector.

Resettlement projects frequently create new slums, and the cleared areas fill up again rapidly. The reiterated complaint everywhere, whether in Manila, Bangkok, São Paulo, or Caracas, is the impossible strain of added commuting costs, often devouring more than one-fourth of the minimum daily wage. This separation of home and job is no clever device, but once again food is taken for granted. How and from where it is to come and at what cost is not considered. Food prices in these far-off settlements are often up by one-fifth or more.

Some of these shanty towns, particularly in Latin America, disappear through police action with or without substitute settlements. Clearing the "favelas" of Rio de Janeiro has been one of the most dramatic of local operations. The authorities worked against time and the constant threat of devastating tropical rains that could wash down shacks and people in avalanches of muddy debris. After six years of slum clearance efforts, there are now only half a million slum dwellers in Rio de Janeiro, which represents a 50 per cent reduction since the task was started. In 1971 the city eliminated 27 shanty towns and moved their dwellers to newly constructed apartments and houses. But even as this slum clearance proceeds, new blighted areas are springing up with the continuing flow of migrants from the interior. In late 1971 it was suddenly discovered that such slums had been created in the hillside woods not far from the presidential palace. Similar incidents of human misery have been reported from around the world. Their counterparts are the "slum-clearances" of the affluent world, which leave space for banks, high-cost apartment buildings, or, at best, low-cost middle class housing, while the truly needy vanish from the picture or are forgotten.

As long as cities are regarded as a by-product of the total action of society's economic and social forces, and as long as these forces are essentially out of balance, cities are bound to become the areas where all of the complications meet, clash, and finally explode.

What are these complications? First, too many people! Cemeteries, antheaps, and rabbit hutches are poor symbols for human progress. Secondly, there are too few jobs. In no way has any development program caught up with the number of urban migrants, with the result that a large proportion have become non-employable and not merely unemployed. The key factors of too many people and too few jobs are coupled with too little capital, too much unskilled labor, stagnant farming, high-cost industry, small markets, and a large-scale technology which neglects the basic needs of man. It is imperative to stem the tide and to introduce population control.

As a rule, cities offer less space, less daylight, less fresh air, less greenery, and more noise. Old, established patterns of communal living are disrupted, and various adjustment problems arise. Undoubtedly psychosomatic and neurotic disorders are largely associated with the congestion and noise, the hectic rhythm of city life, and its vast anonymity. As a kind of compensation, the modern city is supposed to offer employment possibilities and educational facilities and to allow cultural achievements. But cities also specialize in delinquency, crime, prostitution, alcoholism, and drug abuse.

Urbanization of the Affluent World

In the meantime, urbanization moves full speed ahead in the affluent world, which will add only half as many people (195 million) in the 1970's as the poor world, but thereby reducing the numbers in rural areas by another 40 to 50 million. Despite these more modest dimensions, few countries in the well-to-do world show evidence of handling the situation adequately. As the ghettos widen, maintenance is neglected, allowing water, sewage, and power services to deteriorate. Public transit is failing, and private transportation is clogged. Air and water are overloaded as countermeasures fail to keep pace with the mounting volume of pollutants and waste.

Western-Style Traditional Urbanization

The degree of urbanization has frequently been used as a measure of modernization, largely because of the pattern for development suggested by 18th, 19th and early 20th century Western experience. Cities grew in response to the forces of industrialization. The bulk of man's work was removed from the fields and taken into the workshops of early manufacturing. As the factory system grew and railways expanded in its wake, large concentrations of people and services for production and distribution proved economically irresistible. They provided the basis for expanding economies and a broader range of employment. As the whole society became more sophisticated, a widening range of tertiary services was created. In this way cities came to be seen as essential and successful creations and the transmission belts of a new technological system.

It cannot be stressed often enough that what came first was *not* the large cities but the stimulus for industrialization, which induced employment. As 19th-century Europe crossed the threshold of industrialization, the proportion of the population living in cities of more than 20,000 was invariably smaller than the proportion of the working force engaged in manufacturing. In 1856 the percentages in France were 10.7 per cent in the urban areas, with 29 per cent working in industry; for Sweden in 1890, 10.8 and 22 per cent; and for Austria in the same year, 12 and 30 per cent. Switzerland, with its remarkable system of decentralization and cantonal development, produced an even sharper contrast: 45 per cent of its labor force was already in manufacturing, but only just over 15 per cent of the nation were town-dwellers.

Implosion and Deplosion

As the affluent world continues to crowd into cities and in the name of efficiency to create new ones, more and more industrial mass production plants are being built. This development in turn forces even more people to live closer together, both in work and at home. On the whole the population "explosion" and man's burgeoning numbers are behind the rapidly aggravating pollution disturbances, but chiefly through the flow of more people into less space. Demographers have designated this phenomenon *implosion.*

Suburban areas also show a far greater population density per square mile than abandoned farm lands. During and after World War II in both the United States and Europe, a reverse trend, in which the exodus from city centers spread into innumerable suburban development areas, dominated the picture — a happening termed *deplosion.* This process, however, only seemingly reduced the pressure exercised by the congested millions who had flocked to the cities after the mechanization of agriculture. Besides, this trend already is showing signs of a new reversal as the drawbacks of suburban living surface. Many people, particularly those who have raised a family, have moved back to the cities to reduce commuting and to facilitate day-to-day living.

Urbanization of the Poor World

In the present developing world the percentage of the population in towns is considerably higher than that of men working in industry. In 1965 the percentages for Brazil were 32 and 12; Venezuela has the fantastic contrast of 51 and 10 per cent. In 1967 Malaysia and Korea had more than 25 per cent in towns, but just under 10 per cent in industry. Similar figures can be quoted from a number of other nations. Of the larger countries only India was more or less in balance, but is now beginning to show similar disproportions.

These are desperate warning signals of the true nature of today's urban crisis in the developing world. In contrast to the 19th-century experience of Europe and North America, most cities in the developing world exist, as it were, ahead of the industrial system. They lack the manufacturing jobs which, despite their drudgery and misery, gave growing cities a solid base for economic life a hundred years ago.

The Employment Mirage

So far, no employment plan comes even close to caring for the millions presently dumped in the urban slums. In the 1970's some 280 million more will be added to the global labor force. No less than 226 million of these will belong to the less-developed world, a figure three times the total labor force of the United States. Not only will they vastly swell already crowded ranks of underemployed and unemployed, but they will boost even further the number of unemployable millions.

The job supply is quite inadequate in the new cities and threatens to grow more so. Estimates made recently by the Inter-American Development

Bank suggest that on an average 30 per cent of the labor force in Latin American countries is underemployed or unemployed, and that the bulk of this unemployment is among landless men located either in the slums and shanty towns or on the move to the cities. India's fourth 5-year plan (1969-74) estimated that while 19 million new jobs would be created, 23 million more workers would try to enter the labor force. More than 10 million Indians already are officially out of work.

In the big cities there are so-called tertiary activities. Ironically, this index of "high" development renders a larger "tertiary sector" in Latin America than in the United States. But upon closer examination this turns out to be the petty hawking, shoe-shining, message-running type of employment which keeps a man from absolute starvation, but contributes nothing toward the individual's acquisition of skills and confidence or to economic development in general.

The cities of the developing world have outgrown their own means of livelihood. The wretched slums and shanty towns, the steady growth of unemployment, the overloading of the city structure with more and more non-employables, the despairing mothers and semi-starved children — these are all symptoms of a deeper crisis. They have been interpreted as an inability of the cities to adequately realize a full modernization. Yet it is thought that only cities constitute an effective training ground for modern skills and provide a relevant education. But in most regards the traditional urbanization pattern of the West is an outmoded model. To picture what is happening as a forceful thrust toward progress is a verbal crime, since we well know that the dire prerequisites of food and water are grimly missing, and suffocation from a lack of waste disposal or recycling is close at hand (see Chapter 9).

Export Cities

The inherited pattern for commercial exchange between developed and developing peoples — still little modified or adjusted — consists of raw materials from mines and plantations in return for capital and manufactured goods. The developing peoples' share in world trade in manufactures is still only slightly above 10 per cent. This kind of exchange has had a double impact upon urban migration, producing large cities ahead of any basic transformation of the local economy.

To a notable degree the cities of the developing world have been export cities, ports built to dispatch raw materials to Europe and North America and to receive and distribute manufactured goods in return. Rio de Janeiro, Buenos Aires, Santiago, Lagos, Dar-es-Salaam, Bombay, Calcutta, Bangkok, Djakarta, Canton, and Shanghai all had become cities and magnets for migration before even 5 per cent of the people had moved out of subsistence agriculture. In Latin America, where the trend had been intensified by a lively urban tradition in colonial times, the proportion of people in very big cities in 1920 was as high as in developed Europe. Today the proportion is actually above the European level.

The Enigma of Subsistence Farming

The mass movement to the big cities in the poor world is due less to urban attraction than to the pull of employment. Even though such opportunities might be non-existent, many believe they are there. But the overwhelming driving force is harsh rural repulsion resulting from an unbearable degree of overfilling of farms and villages. In the United Kingdom and in most of Europe, two vital changes preceded the expansion of industry, namely the sharp increase in farm productivity and the radical break with feudalism. At least for a time both kept people on the land, either as productive workers or as owners-farmers.

The notion persists that cities created and stimulated farm production, and there are several cases that seem to support this idea. Such examples are frequently picked from Western Europe and Japan, where rural productivity sometimes ensued from city affluence; however, it should be obvious that this could happen only where a margin in land, water, and other development potentials existed.

It is equally true that few of these countries were truly self-sufficient. British urbanization would have been an impossibility without a major flow of food and feed from the North American prairie. The same is still more obvious in Japan. As we have seen, the Netherlands, ever since medieval days, has been a net-importing country in agricultural terms. In a broader sense the urbanizing poor world possesses no such safety valves. It is also a historical fact that the United Kingdom's impressive rate of industrial growth from 1820 to 1950 did not create full employment. The migration to North America provided added job opportunities.

The crucial nature of the urbanization in the poor world centers around the prevalence of subsistence farming and gross inadequacies in commercial farm production both as to magnitude and marketing channels. In far too many instances the subsistence farms were not capable of supporting the rural population even before the population explosion entered the scene. If the added millions were to remain on the land, they would be hard set to stave off hunger. Therefore, they are flocking into the cities in despair, trusting industrialization or other alleged city miracles, sometimes attracted by the hearsay rumors of stored food or incoming deliveries of purchased grain.

Conventional wisdom sees the solution to this dilemma in the modernization of agriculture, completely overlooking such hampering factors as scanty land resources, often less than half an acre per person, the vagaries of climate, the constraints of water, and the harsh ecological framework. The main issue, however, is the great energy input required for fertilizers, irrigation, and distribution (see Chapter 8). In key areas forests have been ransacked out of existence to obtain fuel. That four-fifths of the forest harvest in these lands ends up as fuel should be reason for serious concern. In addition, more wood is extracted illegally from plantations and natural reserve areas. A drastic new deal should give these two-thirds of mankind their share of the fossil fuels.

The fact remains that today's subsistence farmers manage to provide only two-thirds of the food they themselves need, yet it is tacitly assumed that suddenly they shall feed cities of multi-millions in addition. The big urban trek changes nothing in man's dependence on the land but adds tremendously to the cost of food by superimposing heavy distribution, storage and processing burdens. Urban proliferation, therefore, emerges as the core issue in the food-and-people syndrome. The current grim race is too cruel. Far too many millions are in jeopardy, and urbanization is nothing but a hoax.

Only China seems to have faced up to the issue. In the initial phases of the Mao regime, it experienced the most intense urbanization of any country in any period in history. It was not long, however, before the brakes had to be applied. Fifteen to 20 million were forced back to the countryside from the big cities, and further urban expansion was heavily restricted. These acts are a key to China's apparent success in feeding her millions. This made it possible to organize subsidiary feeding through the regional recycling of waste and sewage as a basis for hog and poultry production as well as for fish cultivation. A similar arrangement concentrated to cities would have required costly new investments in food producing sewage plants and fertilizer plants.

Head-On Land Collision

There is an ill-conceived contradiction between the squeeze of the cities and the voracious gobbling of land. According to all logic, the congestion should create large, empty spaces of abandoned rural lands. But cities need agriculture for their feeding. There is an indirect competition between the two, and often they are in direct collision. Cities and suburbs are insatiable and often gobble farms, many of which are first-rate in soil classification. In addition to homes, cities require land for schools, hospitals, industries, airfields, and highways. The Santa Clara Valley, which once was the prime source of California's fruit production, has been almost completely transformed in less than 25 years. In 1941 the county of Los Angeles had 2.65 million people, with 300,000 acres of tilled land, a ratio of 9 to 1. By

1954 there were around 5 million residents, but only 225,000 acres in agriculture. By 1975 the ratio of 9:1 in 1941 will have shot up to 133:1. These figures add up to more than a numbers game in land squeeze.

For a limited time, only land-rich countries like the United States and Canada can endure this kind of land cannibalism. In squeezed Europe and Japan, as well as in other overpopulated regions of the world, this head-on collision between land and people is ominous. The naive hope that remaining lands will compensate for this shrinking acreage is not fulfilled even under the best of circumstances. Such a hope is particularly illusive in western Europe (the Netherlands, Denmark, Switzerland, West Germany) and Japan, where yields already have reached record levels in global terms. Only through outside purchases of food and feed has the illusionist trick of urbanism been performed.

For the 175,000 consumers added each month in the United States, almost 3.5 million new acres need to be brought into cultivation to uphold present dietary standards or a corresponding increase in yield level. In addition farming lands also need to supply feed (hay, grain, and pasture) for the following numbers of added livestock:

Beef cattle	42,500	Hogs	48,000
Dairy cows	26,500	Egg-laying hens	1,350,000
		Broilers	530,000

For the time being the United States still holds a margin, (1) in lands, not fully utilized, (2) in the Soil Bank, and (3) in the potential for higher yields. These are added reasons why we frequently misjudge these matters. Our vantage point is favorably unique for the reasons outlined in Chapter 1 and Chapter 3, p. 40.

Feeding the Megalopoli

Most large cities persistently grow larger and coalesce into huge megalopoli. Before the year 2000 it is anticipated that most of the United States' population will be located in 15 such giant structures, one from Boston to Washington (Boswash), another bridging Detroit with Chicago. Another structure of this sort is appearing in Japan, spanning from Tokyo to Kyoto, as the lowlands are quickly filling up to accommodate some 80 to 90 million people.

Little or no consideration is being given to feeding the large cities in man's immediate future. Proposals are put forward about having huge cargo helicopters land on high-rise structures, about piping in most food in fluid form, or about creating an electronically directed subterranean delivery system of tube conduits. But these ideas are more speculative than constructive and certainly not practical in view of all those for whom food is already prohibitive in price.

While food is almost entirely absent in studies on the emerging megalopoli, even less recognized are the ensuing mountains of sewage and the huge demands for water from the limited recipients within reach. As Chapter 9 will show, most cities of traditional size have failed on both these counts and are faced with enormous new investment demands. In several instances the complications and obstacles appear almost insurmountable.

Only a few key aspects can be indicated here. Each adult requires about 1 lb. of digestible nutrients per day, which amounts to at least 1.5 lbs. of food, and when packaged, some 2 lbs., of which water will average one-fifth. Milk contains even more water. For instance, a million gallons of milk represents 850,000 gallons of water. Existing water pipe systems would obviously distribute this water far more efficiently than tank trucks and at an infinitely lower price. The value of the present trend toward the sale of more milk solids is underlined here. Milk in plastic bottles or cartons has increased its net weight by one-third. This example not only indicates the essentiality of food processing, but also warns us that the seemingly rich choice of alternatives will be narrowed considerably when we have to face up to the overwhelming force created by human numbers.

This leads to a consideration of the growing distance between the fields producing food and feed and the consumers' tables. What is gained in more economic production threatens to be swallowed by marketing costs, particularly those for packaging and transportation. So far the affluent world has managed to carry these debit posts, but only by utilizing extravagant inputs of energy (see Chapter 8). The transfer of animal production into huge units closer to consumer centers is another trend which seems highly dubious, since the transport volume for feed is at least five and even ten times greater than that of the corresponding final products of meat, milk, and eggs.

Supermarkets have grown in size with cities. So have the distances consumers are forced to travel to reach and carry daily food, not to mention the lengthy walks in these temples of Mercurius. The dominating trend towards giant supermarkets appears to have taken very little cognizance of the traffic issue. Community investments for access roads and parking lots, to say nothing of the fuel costs to the consumer, all add to the hidden costs in food. In addition, trucking these huge loads of food into the big cities is already a problem, even when restricted to night hours.

If megalopoli are to be efficiently served, new methods will have to be designed. Traditional deliveries by cars or trucks presumably will have to end at the urban fringes, where conveyor belts or underground tube conduits will take over. Eventually many bulk items in the form of convenience foods will have to be heavily restricted. With this will follow a collectivization of human feeding of dimensions yet unknown; eating at home will be reserved for special occasions or for the more privileged. The practice of eating-out is already gaining ground on a major scale, amounting in the

United States to nearly one-third of all meals. It remains to be seen whether this entire development will end with central kitchens taking over, or whether individual packaging for snack eating or simple home preparations will predominate.

The whole issue, however, cannot be resolved only in the extravagant terms of the affluent world. It is already a far too excruciating matter to the hundreds of millions swarming into cities that cannot absorb them, far less provide for them. The subsidiary costs tower as almost insurmountable when adding up the investments and expenses of transportation facilities (highways and trucks) and marketing, covering the whole range from storage warehouses, processing and packaging to retail outlets. So far most cities in the developing world have slid away, resorting to improvised, makeshift arrangements. Directly coupled with this is the sewage disposal, an indispensable but forgotten link. By what kind of miracles are these millions, overflowing from lands that cannot feed them, suddenly to be provided for, especially since the number of consumers in the producing rural areas also is mounting? Money can do little in this dilemma. Even if in theory their purchasing power were elevated, and even if food for traditional export-import cities came in from the outside, all the subsidiary activities would falter. Development planning has looked at this issue in far too narrow a scope, as simply a question of food and people. Once again we discover the broader ramifications of this fundamental relationship. Confronting the food-and-people dilemma involves infinitely more than raising food or counting people.

Escape into Metaphysics

Faced with this mounting crisis, we delve into the metaphysics of urban planning, smothered in all kinds of unrealistic phraseology. An orgy of terms like ekistics, ecumenopolis, megalopoli and others clutter our thinking. We are avoiding coming to grips with the essentials of housing, schooling, hospitals, water and food provision, and transportation.

Making designs of monstrous human anthills is no effective remedy, whether they are randomized, such as Habitat 67 displayed at the World Expo in Montreal in 1967, or form heaven-reaching cones two miles high and 20 miles in circumference, or are subaquatic cities anchored to the ocean bed, such as Unabara in Japan. These innovations are of little consolation to the wretched masses dumped in the millions like "worn-out cars on mammoth-sized rubbish heaps."

Fancy projects housing 30 to 40 million are of little avail if food and water are not available. Our lack of foresight and our quaint priorities have resulted in a quarter-million dollars going into the researching and developing of a single astronaut meal, but there is hardly a trace of programming, planning, designing, or researching for ways to feed these giant cities of 20 to 30, even 50, million people in our immediate future. This is the great challenge of our days, but it is now so late in the game that to meet the catastrophe will require an emergency plan coupled with a crash program at least on a par with our space efforts.

The creators of fanciful structures for future megalopoli pretend that they are planning with the population explosion and the depopulation of the countryside in mind. They claim they are designing not just for the next decade, but for the next century. They claim they are working out configurations for megalopoli that will allow for "continuous expansion" without producing intolerable congestions around a static center. This new approach, termed "ekistics," supposedly promises future generations the prospect of mastering megalopoli, instead of being victimized by them.

Yet, however vigorously and skillfully this new art may be developing, massive congestion is bound to be the result of the imminent tripling or quadrupling of the earth's population. It is about time we segregated the feasibility and viability from the loftiness of our programming. Above all, we need to master the basic needs of food and water. When judged against the reality of the situation, however, the prospects of success are not good.

The overwhelming driving forces behind this sordid menace in the developing world are the unbearable conditions and meager opportunities in the rural areas. It is a tragic fallacy to compare what is happening there with the previous city growth of the industrializing West. Furthermore, in most writings the role of food in this issue is taken for granted. In addition, employment and education tasks are of such dimensions that they almost fail comprehension, yet it is not recognized that few countries of the developing world have only a fraction of the resources required to adequately employ these millions, much less to provide schooling. The result is both economic and educational stagnation. To find new ways of teaching these masses is truly a challenge to technology. We are witnessing a great historical transformation, in which irrepressible forces are remaking the entire social fabric. These surging waves represent tons of social TNT. Proposals to cope with this dilemma fail on most counts, and are, to say the least, murky, lofty speculations. Most programs are woefully inadequate and far too tardy to be really useful. Besides, in most instances they are almost meaningless as remedial measures.

The British historian Arnold Toynbee visualizes a future world in the following terms: "We are fast moving into a so far barely imaginable new world in which the largest surviving open spaces will be the airports for supersonic aircraft. There will be no room left for traffic on the surface. Goods that are too heavy to be carried by air will have to be transported underground. There will be no room left, either, for agriculture on land: Streets and houses will occupy every acre of terra firma. Food production, if

not fibre production, will be driven out to sea."* When men of Toynbee's
otherwise impressive vision also fall into the urban trap, the situation seems
even more frightening.

* Toynbee, *Change and Habit — The Challenge of Our Time*, 1966, p. 210.

Chapter 8

The Energy Swindle

Man has roamed the earth for perhaps a million years and during the last few thousand years has achieved a modest control of his immediate environment and some degree of security. Within the last half century, however, he has learned to use energy in concentrated form, and, more frightening, in less than two or three centuries he will have used up most of the fossil fuels that have been stored for several hundred million years. In man's early stages human muscles, wood, charcoal, water, and animal power supplied all of his energy, but we are far past that point now. Half of all the fuel ever burned by man has been consumed during the past 50 years.

For a minority of the world's population, the "energy revolution" has created an undreamed-of level of living, has permitted the accumulation of wealth, and has provided enough time and money to allow for the pursuit of science and technology. Less recognized, however, is the fact that food production has become increasingly dependent on a similar massive use of energy, thus diminishing the net gain. Everyone knows that cars and airplanes are run by fuel, but how many realize that more than one-third of the human family maintains itself through food gained by fuel? Even experts are sometimes ignorant in this regard. The public has been given scant opportunity to do other than take its daily food for granted, as conventional information is seriously fragmented and directed mostly to advertising efforts.

Energy Input
for Food Production

The direct input of fossil fuel into food production has indeed a very brief history. It really first began in the 1840's when fuel-powered ships brought fertilizers (guano and later, bone meal) from South America to Europe, primarily to the United Kingdom. Coal was not used to power fishing vessels or trains until the latter part of the 19th century. After 1910 transportation vehicles relied almost exclusively on fossil fuels. Most agriculture functioned without the input of outside fuel until almost 1860 in Europe and 1900 in North America. The direct use of fuel in agriculture started with the manufacturing of fertilizers after 1922. The striking feature of these developments is for how brief a period fossil fuels have operated behind the food scene. From being a novelty 130 years ago, they have reached significant proportions only in the last half-century, becoming a truly driving force after World War II.

Two Basic Fallacies

In *The Hungry Planet*, published by this author in 1965, attention was drawn to two basic fallacies prevalent in the appraisal of agricultural production in the Western world. One was the quaint practice of matching output to man-hours and not taking into account the big input of energy. No industrialist in charge of a fully automatized plant would think of crediting his output to the single man pushing the buttons which control operations. The other fallacy was the failure to recognize the nature of the alleged agricultural revolution and the completely changed nature of the farmer's task. Much of what he traditionally did has been moved from the farm site to entirely new sectors of productive functions, involving the services of many city-dwellers. No man really feeds 75,000 chickens daily all by himself. Rather he is aided by those who make the equipment, raise the grain, process and package the feed, make and install the feed conveyor belts, and perform other related services. The U.S. Department of Agriculture states that in 1947, 5 million people were engaged in supplying farmers. By 1965 this figure had risen to 7 million.

From Labor-Intensive
to Capital-Intensive

The basic change behind the food scene is the conversion of Western agriculture from a labor-intensive to a capital-intensive status, with the United States leading the transformation. Although the number of operational farms has been reduced, their size has grown, as evidenced by the unchanged total of tilled acreage. Machinery is the greatest and most costly factor in this process. Despite a constant acreage, the value of farm machinery in the United States has almost tripled in 11 years (1954-65), from 12.1 to 34.2 billion dollars, and the value of power-driven spraying machines has doubled.

The use of farm machinery, fertilizers, and spray chemicals has greatly increased the volume of production on each farm and has brought many advantages to society. The true costs, however, have largely been measured in terms of gains and benefits. Losses and handicaps are rarely registered or added to present a balanced account. The direct and indirect impact of agricultural technology on the environment and on societal structures has only been vaguely assessed. This chapter will not venture into providing such a complete, balanced account, but rather will direct its attenton to energy, which is crucial to man's future.

Mechanization (Motorization)

Farm efficiency culminated in mechanization, or more specifically tractorization, or motorization. It is almost unbelievable that in 1850 two-thirds (65%) of all work was performed through the muscle power of men and animals. Even as late as 1920, more than 20 million horsepower (hp) was actually provided in the United States by horses and mules.

Tractors and Man-hours in U.S. Agriculture

	Tractors (million hp)	Man-hours (billion)
1920	5	13.4
1950	93	6.9
1960	154	4.6
1969	203	3.4

In the United States farm tractors now prevail and consume 8 billion gallons of fuel annually, equivalent to more than one thousand trillion British Thermal Units (BTU's) of heat energy (1969). Thus through tractors the average American burns 4.5 million BTU's per year or 32 gallons of gasoline per capita. The energy value of the food crops, therefore, must include the amount of energy burned in tractors as well as all the other energy items of a regular farm budget.

Electricity is also used in considerable amounts on farms, increasing fivefold between 1940 and 1965. In 1969 the generation of such electricity for farms through thermoelectrical plants required almost 2 million BTU's for each United States citizen, a figure equivalent to 14 gallons of gasoline per capita.

As early as the mid-19th century, researchers pointed out that most agricultural efforts to induce higher "artificial" yields of food would involve considerable expenditure of energy, both in the manufacture and transport of fertilizers as well as in the cultivation of soil and the control of weeds.

Energy Use of U.S. Farms Per Year, 1969
(per U.S. citizen)

	Million BTU'S	Equivalent in gallons of gasoline
Tractors	4.5	32
Fertilizers	5.72	40
Electricity	2.0	14
Other uses	15.2	106

Currently, for the cultivation of each acre of land, an energy input of 10 million BTU's is required, or put another way, the feeding of each American requires the equivalent of 150 gallons of fuel per year. This constitutes five times more energy than the amount actually contained in the food consumed. Yet this figure includes neither the energy expended in making the farm equipment nor the critical costs of storing and marketing the food. The energy required to make the steel, rubber, paint, and other commodities necessary for this huge machinery should also be added to the farm budget.

Energy and Food, 1969 (A)
(per capita)

	Food			Total Energy in Farm Production			
	Kcal/ day	Kcal/ year (million)	Kg CE*	Kg CE	Food (per cent)	Fuel on farm** Kg CE	Fertilizer KgCE†
U.S.A.	11,910	4,350	635	10,774	5.9	165	210
Japan	5,494	2,000	292	2,828	10.3	15	112
Taiwan	4,762	1,742	254	874	29	na	89
India	2,896	1,059	154	193	80	na	15

* Coal equivalents.
** Fossil fuel used on farms (not electricity).
† In manufacturing (not transportation).

The average American daily consumes 3,300 calories; this amount, however, represents about 12,000 calories of input. About 10,000 calories per capita per day are required as an input into livestock to produce the animal products (meat, milk, and eggs) consumed. Judged in this manner, each acre involved in the production of food or feed receives an input of energy roughly equal to the energy which crops capture through photosynthesis, a relationship which places in great question the basic energy economy of modern agriculture.

Many more examples can be given to substantiate this kind of imbalance. For instance, soybean-producing Iowa farms are using up more fuel per acre than the calories carried in the harvested soybeans; the amplitude is 2.35 to 3.5 times. Many dairy farms, on the same amount of acreage, are using three to five times more energy than ever could be raised through crops. Whaling also has been cited as an example of energy inconsistencies, as each whaler brought home in whale oil only 1/8th to 1/12th of the total amount of fuel used by the ship. Of course these expenses may well have been justified, for besides oil the whaler brought back glandular treasures and meat. And it must be remembered that the soybean is an invaluable protein source. Nevertheless, we should know the total cost of our food bill, particularly since the energy account presumably will creep upward from now on.

The Marketing Bill

Urbanization has added still another major cost factor to the food bill. Processing and packaging are persistently demanding greater attention, as man has gone a long way from the days when small cities and villages were easily served by adjacent farmlands. Transportation and marketing have become dominants, both in price structure and in energy demands. In 1969 the energy demands in the United States were as follows:

U. S. Energy Use for Transportation and Marketing of Food, 1969
(Kg CE per capita)

Primary energy in food	Energy on the farm	Energy used in processing and marketing
635	1,010*	652**

* See Table 37.
** Transportation is 55 to 60% of this total.

As this table indicates, we have evidently created a third sector, which is persistently growing in pace with the congregation of humans. An unexpected consequence of the concomitant specialization of farming is that even farmers depend on the same vast delivery system. If projected onto the global scene, however, one can seriously question whether this model or pattern is feasible in the Hungry World. Can the rest of the world allow itself the energy and resource feast implied in these trends? Can we in the affluent world continue to burden our food accounts with these huge extra charges? When viewed in this manner, our frivolity is stupendous.

Complete Energy Accounting

Many textbooks make the statement that the energy encased in food represents a very small and actually diminishing fraction of the energy consumed in fuel and electricity. In most instances, the food energy itself has been computed incorrectly. When measured on the basis of the calorie content within the food as it is actually eaten, food does rate rather low in energy, particularly in developed countries. But this is a highly misleading figure since it neglects to include all the calories required to raise that food (App. Table 35). In the case of animal products, there are also considerable conversion losses. Animal product calories have to be multiplied by a conversion factor of seven (1:7).

The difference in calories per capita per day between the United States and India is therefore not 3,300 to 1,900 (App. Table 36), but actually more than seven times larger: 11,900 to 2,910. Instead of 1,400 kcal per person it is 8,990 calories, an awesome discrepancy which illuminates a much overlooked aspect of the food-and-people issue. It is not sufficient to count heads or to add up calories in the food eaten. In any kind of valid comparison the nutritional standard grossly affects both. In addition, this example illustrates how much less it takes to keep an East Indian going than an American. Such data also opens up entirely new vistas on basic economic relationships, such as personal income, salaries, and expenditures.

Next comes the vital question of what additional inputs of calories precede consumption? Here the input of power and fuel on the farm must be considered. Since available data do not allow a broad analysis of various countries, attention has been limited to the fertilizer account (App. Table 37). No consideration has been given to the substantial amounts of energy needed to manufacture spray chemicals and to process feed, nor to the power used on the farm, all of which are a substantial part of the energy-demanding items in modern agriculture.

In this context the relative standing of food is much larger than most textbooks imply. Yet it remains true that in developed countries food is on a descending scale, a trend which changes the picture considerably when a more accurate energy accounting is introduced. Even the energy involved in the manufacture of fertilizers appreciably boosts the energy base behind food, a factor which applies not only in well-to-do countries, which generally show a high input of fertilizers, but also in poor countries, many of which import considerable amounts of fertilizers for plantation crops, such as sugar (Cuba, Reunion, Mauritius, Fiji), bananas (Ecuador, El Salvador), cotton (Egypt, Peru), and others.

Biology and Technocracy

It would be intriguing and presumably rewarding to compare the net gains of the energy revolution in agriculture both in terms of plant and animal protein with the net gains of the biological conquest via nitrogen-fixing bacteria (Fig. 7), each of which has a prerequisite for the effective utilization of Western man's global grasslands booty. One day the complete history of the white clover, alfalfa, and pulses as pivotal influences on

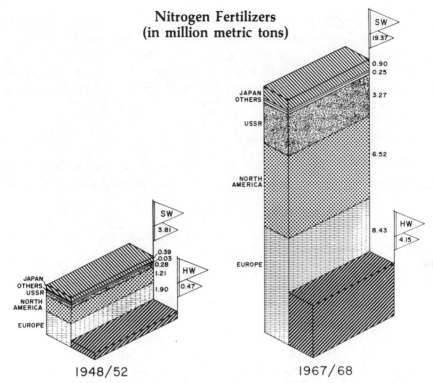

Figure 7:   Growth in the use of commercial nitrogen fertilizers, 1948/52 to 1967/68, divided between the Satisfied World (SW) and the Hungry World (HW). Note the much bigger increase in usage by the Satisfied World (SW).

animal production and protein provision will be written. The grand show of oilseeds also belongs in this picture. Considered in long-range perspective, these developments may well turn out to be far more significant to man's feeding than the indiscriminate energy squandering. For example, five tons of coal are required to manufacture one ton of nitrogen. Phosphates are mineralized through microorganisms at a much lower cost through phosphate plants. In both cases nature operates in a far more economizing manner than man as burdensome transportation costs are not involved. Many of the traditional ideas of Western man need to be tested against the basic laws of thermodynamics. Man also needs to take some lessons in operational economics from living nature.

There happens to be a tinge of parody to all the praise lavished on man's accomplishments in marshalling the photosynthetic riches of the plant kingdom and on his ingenious unleashing of the constraints on the energy-catching mechanism and devices of the green plant. Man's input of energy on behalf of his "tricks" is extraordinary. While one might argue that this is a reasonable price to pay for the invaluable fringe benefits of special fats and protein, it is far more essential to realize that this practice places the future of this kind of agricultural operation in jeopardy. On the day when the supply of fossil fuels comes to an end, whether this happens within one or three hundred years, some far more sensible device will desperately be needed. Recognizing the free, lavish flow of sun energy, it obviously will not pay to earmark a whole acre of land for energy delivery (via sugar cane or sugar beet) for each acre of specialized crop production.

Budget Revision Needed

Man's basic budget will need drastic revision as the supply of fossil fuels diminishes. Those civilizations which have grasped the significance of true economy will have the greatest chance of survival — not the squanderers or hoarders, but the efficient operators. It is sobering to recognize that in terms of maximum return per input of energy, many poor countries rank far ahead of affluent ones.

Once again only a minority of the human family has reaped the benefits of the one-time trick of mechanization. The vast acreages gained by substituting the iron horse for the real horse are only feeding some 400 million people. When this glorious film of abundance is replayed under the flickering light of parsimony, there will be a grim awakening, and the great energy swindle will come to an end. When the fairytales vanish, all of mankind once again will be on an equal footing.

There is nothing wrong in using these rich energy sources. The crime rests in not following a budget, in not recognizing their non-renewable nature, and in seriously believing that this energy-gorging is the inalienable privilege of a select minority. For more than a century we were convinced that this orgy could be shared, and we circled the globe in an almost evangelistic crusade for world salvation on that fragile assumption. Mankind is travelling, as it were, in a fire-balloon far above the normal equilibrium level, and sooner or later it must descend, at the latest when heat or energy derived from fossil fuels runs out. The excessive energy use by the well-to-do world may therefore be nothing more than a grand-scale swindle, creating an empty purse for the Hungry World.

Some people pray for nuclear energy as our savior, but we are certainly far better advised to tap the rich flow of sun-energy. Twenty-five years after the atom bomb, nuclear energy accounts for only less than one per cent of the world's energy production. This is not a net figure, however, as the huge inputs of fossil fuel employed in producing nuclear fuel have not been subtracted. Furthermore, nuclear energy can take the place of only about one-fifth of our present usage, which is heavily geared toward mobile needs. It also seems that nuclear waste and effluents are rapidly reaching unmanageable proportions. This issue is extremely critical, yet the U.N. Conference on the Environment, held in Stockholm in 1972, not only refused to place the matter on its agenda, but did not even venture to listen to an expert analysis of the pending crisis.

The Energy Gap

The Hunger Gap has its counterpart in an Energy Gap, which is becoming larger at an ever-increasing rate (App. Table 34.) The well-to-do nations, comprising only 28 per cent of the world population, are feverishly extending their lead, using 85 per cent of all energy consumed. Several of these countries show an annual increase in fuel and energy consumption far greater than the total use in most nations below the world's poverty line.

These staggering discrepancies can be formulated in terms of numbers of people. Employing primary calories as a measuring rod, the United States figures per capita and per day are four times larger than those of India, which means that 830 million people could be accommodated within the United States if restricted to the per capita level of India (both computed on the basis of their respective per capita energy use in food). (App. Table 35).

Considering all resources, energy consumption in the United States (1969) was approximately 21 times greater, corresponding to that of 11.5 billion Indians. And all of these figures need to be doubled in recognition that the average life-span in India is only half of that in the United States. In other words, the United States has created a civilization so extravagant that it could stretch to fill the energy needs of 23 billion Indians. In terms of food, this figure would be 1.6 billion, a fact which throws an entirely new light on traditional population density figures. Judged in terms of total energy consumption, the United States is therefore heavily populated, not sparsely.

Growth Adjustment and New Priorities

The use of resources is growing at a far greater rate than population, currently doubling in 14 years as compared to 30 years for human numbers. As the world population doubles, industrial activities quadruple. Percentage increases in such inputs as fertilizers, pesticides, and power exceed the corresponding gains in yield by 2.5 to 3 times. In other words, intensification of agriculture can be achieved, but only with diminishing returns from increased energy inputs. This is feasible only as long as technological advances enable the cost of these inputs to remain below the value of the product.

When the interactions of agriculture with food processing, transportation, industry, and urbanization are considered, larger populations are forced into more intensive and complex systems in order to survive. Mankind is well along that road already. The romanticized cry of "back to nature" through genuine subsistence coupled with pastoral restoration has come far too late in the game. If the world were to choose such a future, it would find itself grossly overpopulated. About four-fifths of the human race would have to be eliminated if each individual were to have a reasonable supply of resources, and if cultural growth and civilization were to continue to be viewed in energy terms. The world cannot afford its present energy nobility and eventually will be forced to give priority to food and water for survival.

With the present growth rate in world population of about 2 per cent annually, the rate at which we are processing material is increasing about 5 per cent per year. This is an index rate based primarily on resource acquisition and waste production and quite accurately reflects the true cost of population growth. The rate at which we process materials is one measure of the ecological demands mankind is exerting upon the natural environment. With a doubling every 14th year, pollution and environmental deterioration are bound to become critical. This explains why major difficulties have emerged so suddenly. If this processing rate doubles twice more before the end of the century, there is little hope that institutional corrective measures can proceed fast enough to keep up. Recent proposals to limit the hectic economic growth now proceeding on a short-range depletion of non-renewable resources are therefore clearly justified.

Chapter 9

Food In Man's Ecology

In his quest for food, man's impact on the face of earth has been truly formidable. With the aid of fire, the ax and the plow he has profoundly reshaped the world. However, he has created more deserts than he ever irrigated new land; he has cut down more than half of the world's forest cover; he has denuded vast lands, exposing them to the destructive forces of water and wind; and through excessive cropping he has destroyed many times more acres of top-soil than he ever built up or newly produced.

These changes have resulted in large-scale ecological crises — as far back as 3000 years ago in China, around the Mediterranean at the time of Christ, and, finally, in the dry prairies of the United States, culminating in the Dust Bowl catastrophe of 1935. The repercussions of man's changes, which have been felt up until our own time, also include an upset of the water balance, involving desiccation and the alternate formation of marshlands downstream, which in turn have engendered malaria and other water-borne diseases. Often costly drainage has had to be installed or extensive flood control measures placed upstream.

Man also has tapped enormous volumes of groundwater, releasing them to the oceans or atmosphere without replenishment. Presumably he cannot return the vast amounts of water removed through the centuries from underground, nor restore the forests he has pulled down, nor remake the top-soils he has squandered. Most of these developments have climaxed in this century; man is scraping the pot of food and resources, leaving too little to be shared by too many.

Ecological Myopia

This book has already placed the emphasis on a slightly different aspect of these global phenomena, namely the great European migration.

The 100-year outpouring from one of the main centers of overpopulation made its peoples lose touch with the basic realities of their existence. The millions raised in the big cities of North America did not relate to the distant prairie lands or, in the case of Europe, the far away continents on which they depended. All they saw and felt was transformed into abstract money values, and so Western man lost sight of the fact that his survival, despite all technical advancement, hinged upon the vast acreages beyond the horizon.

Such ignorance reflects a colossal blunder of Western education, which promulgated the notion that Western man had opened up the treasure chests of the globe and had transformed the "backward" world into a richly flowing cornucopia. The price tag of eroded and depleted coffee, cotton, and banana lands, the malnourished plantation workers, and the denuded forests was never displayed. How many Europeans ever understood the relationship between the Dust Bowl catastrophe of the prairie and their own appetites, whether they had remained in the old continent or had settled in the new colony of North America!

The great European migration, or the Golden Age of Western Man, was actually a grand-scale mobilization of the globe's remaining grasslands: the prairies, the pampas, the veld and the savannas of Africa and Australia, and the newly created pastures of New Zealand. In the postwar period this great ecological conquest had a repeat performance in the oceans. The marine pastures, the rich plankton areas off the west coasts of South America and South Africa were dipped into, and huge catches of plankton-eating fish were converted into meal and oil. The meal has been moving almost exclusively into Europe and the United States, supporting their animal production, although a minor portion has gone to Japan. The oil has been earmarked for the fat industry of Europe.

Issues Central to Food in Man's Ecology

This chapter also intends to focus attention on some neglected aspects of food in man's ecology. Therefore, only brief allusions will be made to topics traditionally explored. For instance, man has created ever-widening fields for his crops, thus releasing the bounty of the earth to his exclusive benefit. But in the process he has unquestionably raised the risk level from pests and diseases by placing richly laden tables within easy reach of these foes. Man has unwittingly favored these competitors and forced himself into a far more vigorous battle, leading to an all-out chemical warfare which often strikes friend and foe alike. What used to be single, isolated attacks have merged into a constant onslaught, as more and more varieties of rodents, insects, fungi, and bacteria follow upon one another.

Storage of food and feed also has become an indispensable and expanding operation. It was long distance hauling, mainly into the Western world, that greatly contributed to the global spreading of storage insects, often field insects from the warm world, and prompted the birth of fumigation and applied entomology. While these processes are great advances, their very necessity reflects how cavalierly and with what little biological foresight man handled these key matters.

Finally, the most upsetting factor in ecological terms has been the extension of irrigation into a year-round operation. Man did not restrict his technological endeavors to creating monsoon conditions in arid regions. Instead he went one step farther and introduced conditions similar to the humid tropics. This affected the soils and opened the door to a whole spectrum of disease agents and vectors. Unfortunately, man's costly counterinsurgence in preventing the spread of malaria, schistosomiasis, river blindness, and many crop and animal pests and diseases has been only partially successful. Admittedly, this is a very brief sketch, but it should serve as a reminder of some highly significant ecological ramifications of the food-and-people issue.

The Chemical Threat to Food

It is frequently said that man's food is currently threatened by an avalanche of chemicals, perhaps exceeding a half-million compounds. An adjustment of perspective is necessary here; one is reminded that all foods are nothing other than chemicals, or actually the specific combination of chemical nutrients, that, when eaten, must be present simultaneously to allow normal body metabolism.

Since the beginning of this century, the Western world has created through canning, freezing, and refrigeration a major non-chemicalized sector, which comprises the core of daily food. In this way chemical preservatives and toxic compounds, which are formed from molds and other spoilage agents, have been eliminated. Of major significance has been the removal of salt as a preservative (in the annual amount of 50 to 100 lbs. per person) and the subsequent relief to over-taxed kidneys. In the United States the hazards to food do not result from additives employed in the processing and manufacture of food since such additives are not only under strict administrative control but are constantly checked by the control laboratories of industry. Instead, the chemical risks to our foods come from contaminants which may be ranked in the following order:

1. *microbial food poisonings, including mycotoxins, resulting from diverse molds;*
2. *dietary imbalances, creating malnutrition and metabolic disturbances, and evidenced by dental decay and arteriosclerosis;*

3. environmental pollutants (DDT, chlorodioxon, lead, mer-
    cury, cadmium, and so on);
4. imbalances in food composition, created by fertilizers, es-
    pecially nitrogenous ones.

In the developing world mycotoxins constitute a major threat. Some
20 compounds (islanditoxin, ochratoxin, tremortin, aflatoxin, luteoskyrin,
and others) have been identified in such key commodities as cereals and
beans. These elements cause liver damage, induce tumor growth, or exert
metabolic disturbances, in all instances more critically when the victims are
malnourished. Hundreds of millions of people around the world are suscep-
tible, tens of millions are affected, and many millions actually succumb.

Food Flow from Producer to Consumer

Accelerated and pronounced urbanization has profoundly changed
the volume and nature of foods from the producers' fields to the consumers'
tables. Population growth is an intimate part of this picture. United States'
figures illustrate well what has happened all over the Western world.

U.S. Population — 1900 and 1972 (in millions)

Year	Urban	Rural	Total
1900	26	50	76
1972	166	43*	209
Increase	6.3	0.84	2.7 times

* partly suburban

In the United States, where only a minor portion of the population is
directly engaged in providing food for the urbanized millions, the needs of
each and everyone add up to a colossal operation profoundly affecting the
woodlands, ranchlands, streams, lakes and ponds. In other words, food is
the greatest industry of all in our highly technicalized society.

The flow of food into the cities is not only six times greater than at
the turn of the century, but the total intake per capita also has increased
(Fig. 8). This flow has been tempered somewhat by the creation of major
transformers along this food life-line in the shape of food processing industries, shunting off wastes through the trimming of inedible and less-
digestible parts. But these plants for secondary concentration have created
new pollution sources. What were once dispersed rural wastes have now
become highly concentrated ones located in the population center.

We can take little comfort in the fact that the origins of most pollution phenomena can be traced back to the infancy of man and his first steps
toward the conquest of the globe. The current pollution crisis has been

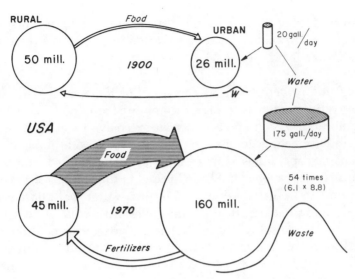

Figure 8: U.S. Urbanization, 1900 to 1970 (in million of people) showing the effect on: distribution of population, urban import of food, waste accumulation, farm deliveries of fertilizers, and domestic use of water per capita.

triggered by the environmental impact of contemporary population concentrations.

From Food to Sewage to Pollution

Most pollution is caused by too many people, resulting in man's disturbing the natural cycling of energy and materials. In an undisturbed natural system, primary producers (chiefly green plants) synthesize their own organic food out of carbon dioxide, water and minerals, using energy from the sun. All other living creatures feed on these plants either directly by grazing or indirectly by consuming the flesh of other creatures who feed on plants. Part of the ingested food is excreted and eventually broken down by bacteria into its inorganic components for reuse by the plants.

In permanent human settlements, however, the man-induced phenomena of solid and liquid wastes become potent. The by-products of human use that in nature would have returned to the cycle immediately as food for other organisms become concentrated out of their wild, natural context and develop into a nuisance. We have been overrating both the cycling capability of nature and its load-carrying capacity.

Civilization has produced more and more sophisticated methods for discarding waste, from a simple hole in the ground to an outhouse, to a septic tank, to a very complex sewage treatment plant. In the process the metabolic cycle has been split more and more widely in both time and space. In the sewage treatment plant, the inorganic components (the end products of the cycle) are produced by a highly controlled microbial system and then discarded into the nearest body of water. As a natural system, the water responds to the higher mineral level by producing more green plants (algae) and a higher level of biological activity, often with massive fluctuations in the birth and death of species.

Recycling Imperative. As the result of the crucial dispersal factor and split operations, human sewage, originating from food, is a major factor in water pollution. When spread over an extensive rural area, the human wastes of a million people do not constitute the same pollution load on water and its cleansing capabilities as when these are concentrated from a city of a million. This simple fact has not been heeded in time and, as a consequence, sewage treatment, indispensable in averting water pollution calamities, shows an alarming backlog in the entire Western world. A corresponding mineral depletion of cultivated soils has led to a vast counterstream of mineral fertilizers moving to the farms. As cities continue to bulge, recycling this waste, presumably by converting sewage plants into food-producing centers, is the only recourse. Algae, yeast, mushrooms, insects, quail, and fish are some of the alternative end-products in such an operation. Research in this area, however, is notoriously slow.

Ancient Pattern — The Road Ahead. In the year 950 the palaces of Angkor, capital of the ancient Khmer empire (in present-day Cambodia), stood in all their majestic grandeur, adorned with marble elephants marching in stone, and with mythical birds, called garudas, holding the balustrades in their upraised claws. It was a humming city, surrounded by extensive fish ponds, the center of a mighty commonwealth which extended all the way from Burma to the South China Sea. All food was raised within the reaches of the city, and the wastes were recycled via the cultivated fish. The whole city was an ideal, balanced ecosystem in which pollution was banished and subsistence assured. Fine gardens and irrigated fields garnished the daily diet with rice, cucumbers, and similar items. Even though these events occurred 100 years before the British Isles were invaded by William the Conqueror, Angkor is still a model socio-ecological system.

Many cities in central Europe and the southern part of the Soviet Union recycle their sewage by cultivating fish in ponds, frequently in combination with the raising of ducks. Several Southeast Asian cities do the same and obtain fine gouramis, carp, and other fish which all feed on worms, plankton and living organisms nourished by the riches of sewage. If we are not to be submerged by excessive expenses, the recycling of organic matter will have to be our future pattern. It is an urgent matter that food be shunted into such production chains.

The Food Balance. Sanitation engineers were the first to introduce the population equivalent concept (abbreviated as PE units), making it possible to gauge the polluting effect of other organic wastes in relation to that of human sewage. Among industrial plants contributing such waste are paper pulp factories, cornstarch manufacturers, fruit and vegetable canners, meat packers, and dairies. Some indication of the major task of this phase can be attained by measuring the polluting effect of selected food industries.

Pollution Effect of Assorted Food Industries

	Reference Quantity	Population Equivalents
Brewery	1 ton beer	50-100
Dairy	1 ton milk	20-200
Fruits & vegetables	1 ton raw product	100-500
Slaughterhouse	1 ton slaughtered animals	100-200*
Sugar	1 ton beets	5-85
Starch	1 ton potatoes	ca. 500

* Depending on size of cattle

This effect is in itself an interesting side aspect to the food-and-people issue. Through its waste disposal each food-processing plant exerts a polluting influence which can be measured in terms of number of people.

In any country both human numbers and the degree of urban congestion determine the amount of water pollution as measured in population equivalents. On that basis reasonable estimates can be made of the degree to which total pollution is critical and the extent to which it is overloading local water recipients. Such an estimate for the United States would look like this:

Water Pollution in the United States (A)
(in million PE units)

1971	Total	Active	Latent*
Man	205	165	40
Livestock	2,000	870	1,136
		(950)	(1,050)
Industry	675	475**	200

* Diluted by nature to reasonable levels with little discernible nuisance.
** Almost half of this linked to food (processing plants, dairies, canneries, packaging plants).

This table conveys one singularly important message — that food processing is a far more potent factor in the current pollution picture than is generally recognized.

Second-time Fertilizing. Even with removal of organic wastes, normally to around 80 per cent, we are still left with most of the minerals, which inevitably mount with human numbers. They are also supported by the fertilizer industry, which keeps the flow of food running at a constantly elevated level. Inescapably this means a second-time fertilizing, not of the fields but of the recipient waters, inducing a rapid resynthesis of the organic matter which has already been removed once in costly treatment procedures. Because of this, a mandatory removal of most organic matter — in principal prohibition against the release of raw sewage — would do little to relieve the water of polluting forces. The ignition and spark plug would still remain. Even with tertiary treatment, costs would prohibit a complete removal of all minerals. Thus, despite such extensive sewage treatment, the pollution load would irrevocably mount with human numbers.

As land, often the very best agricultural soils, are taken for urban expansion, suburban development, or industries and airfields, yields have to be increased on remaining soils. This has become a factor in the mounting fertilizer loads. In particular, nitrogen has become a critical pollution factor because of the strains on the microbial balance system of the soils. In some regions of southern Scandinavia, western Europe, and the midwestern United States, leaching has elevated the nitrogen content of the water draining from the cropland, causing nitrate hazards.

The least understood aspect of the food-and-people issue is these disruptions in mineral cycling, initiated by human settlement and the thrust of agriculture, and culminating almost in disaster in modern, multi-million cities. No one could deny that this entire sequence was perpetrated by the growth in human numbers, a fact particularly true of the latest phase, the creation of megalopoli. It is an exercise in futility to debate whether this should be blamed on the number of people or on technological procedures; they are closely interrelated.

The Wastes from Animal Production. At this point another aggravating and compounding factor enters the scene. At the very same time that man in his cavalier attitude expects nature and its waters to perform miracles and graciously take care of increasing loads, he is almost feverishly depriving nature of available water, overtaxing lakes and rivers, as well as groundwater. Human sewage — ensuing from food — is, however, not the chief culprit, nor are the food processing plants, although they dominate the industrial scene as polluters. The overwhelming issue is the modern, large-scale establishments for animal production: the massive broiler hotels, the hog factories, and above all the feedlots. On the basis of available statistics, this author calculated the waste emanating from such installations to be 870 million PE units. Similar, more recent computations reached a still higher figure (950 million).

In terms of protein intake, the livestock of the United States represent around 1,200 million PE units. But in pollution effect via their excreta, they account for no less than 2 billion PE units. Through such estimates an entirely new vista is gained on the food-and-people relationship or, more precisely, how the consumption level of animal products has profound ecological repercussions. In ecological terms a meat and milk consumer is a far more disturbing element in nature than a bread eater.

Mounting Water Use

Understood far less than the sewage blunder are the broader ramifications of mounting water requirements. In the United States the use of water has climbed drastically, from an average of 20 gallons per person per day (gd.) since 1900 to 180 gd. in 1972. Europe shows about half that figure. Some American cities register a still greater use of water for domestic purposes, such as Chicago (230 gd.) and San Diego (580 gd.). These figures indicate that pollution troubles are further aggravated by the ever-mounting volumes of water that man is withdrawing from lakes, rivers and groundwaters. Water use in industry is also mounting, and to make matters worse, sanitary engineers are still relying on the ancient Roman method of removing human sewage by water, making this single operation a polluter of more water than any other. In this way food indirectly becomes an environmental nuisance — from food to sewage to pollution. Increasingly, and with all the sanitary risks involved, drinkable water has to be recovered for reuse from sewage plants. Despite the use of chlorine, this method is highly questionable as to its efficiency in destroying viruses.

In addition, nature's cleansing capability via natural water recipients has been weakened by a growing thermal pollution, further reducing the oxygen level. The release of toxic chemicals from industry into our waters also taxes nature's cleansing machinery. Thus a whole set of vicious circles emerges from the ecology of man's feeding.

The Oceans in Jeopardy

Sooner or later most pollutants end up in the oceans; some urban and industrial wastes are even shipped out to sea for dumping. The marine environment is already heavily strained by petroleum products and affected by pesticides and chemical fertilizers.

The oceans have always been the common dump of mankind, but the amounts unloaded have not only climbed drastically but have become increasingly hazardous. Although no aquatic organism, man has emerged in the last quarter of a century as not only the most influential animal in the marine sphere, but also as the most destructive. Since more than half of the wastes originate with the developed, oil-ridden world, the situation has broad international implications. Should one-fifth of mankind be allowed to jeopardize the oceans, a life-supporting element for major portions of the globe's peoples?

The United States and most European countries have pledged immediate measures to halt ocean dumping, but how many realize that in its ultimate consequence, this goal will not be achieved without an accompanying end to pollution of inland waters. There is no question that food via sewage has been instrumental in ruining the waters of Lake Erie and major sections of the Atlantic off New York and around Long Island.

Man, a Superfactor

Man has unquestionably become a "superfactor" in the world of living nature. By arbitrarily removing water, especially by drying up its natural flow, he has caused great upheaval in the living world, eradicating many animals, changing their habitats, and affecting practically the entire fauna and flora. Primarily through man's actions, the world's desert acreage has more than doubled since the end of the 1880's. Even the enormous irrigation projects of this century, which have resulted in a fourfold increase of irrigated acreage since 1900, have not been able to balance out these losses. Man now outnumbers by far all other species of major mammals, and he has placed under his domination — merely to obtain food — more than one-fifth of the primary production of the green plant cover.

Seemingly man's power position is well entrenched, but his basis is fragile. Despite his potency and his technological arsenal, man's vulnerability has increased. His rule is faltering because he has not mastered the difficult art of self-restraint. Health and adequate food remain the privilege of a minority, while disease and nutritional deficiency are the destiny of an ever-growing majority. The world's food does not suffice because we have closed our eyes to these biological dimensions and have neglected to look after our house in time. The productive prerequisites of the earth with all its hazards and limitations make it increasingly difficult to meet the needs of mankind. We are already too many, and as a first step toward true progress, we must devote our prime attention to taking care of those *now* living, in lieu of holding out invalid promises about feeding future billions.

New Priorities and Formulas

The ecological consciousness now sweeping the world is basically a sound phenomon. Nevertheless, few seem to realize the complexity and true nature of the environmental crisis. Our biological education is wholly inadequate when it comes to grasping implications concerning overpopulation, pollution, hunger, exploitation, depletion, and the like, except in very simplistic terms. In effect, our whole way of life is in jeopardy. To regain control of man's destiny and to assure survival we have to mend our ways drastically and formulate entirely new goals and priorities.

For far too long we have identified progress with technical novelties and have paid too little attention to the true costs. By willing the means we naively believed that we would attain our goals. Both modern medicine and technology have fallen victim to the false notion that the removal or alleviation of symptoms was sufficient, forgetting the fundamental need for a causal therapy. Much of present-day ecological reasoning falls into this same trap. We shirk from the duty to formulate a meaningful strategy. We

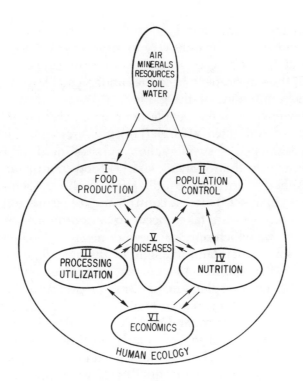

Figure 9:   The Six Factor Model. Key Factors affecting
the Food-and-People relationship.

prefer to indulge in costly tactical maneuverings, hoping for miracles.

Two basic dimensions are missing in the current debate, namely those of history and biology. The present adverse conditions cannot be effectively tackled either in the affluent world or in the developing world, unless we take cognizance of man's prime role as an ecological superfactor. Through the postwar technical aid programs we rambled into the hungry, poor world, seemingly unaware that it once embraced many of the world's advanced civilizations prior to our own. Many were overpopulated, overextended in soils and water, and suffered from excessive deforestation. More than one hundred million persons are in effect ecologically displaced because they are tilling soils that should never have been opened for cropping. It is high time that we acquaint ourselves with the realities of our globe, its history and ecology in the grips of man, and begin to make amends.

Food alone may be the critical factor for man's survival, but more often it is only one of a number of environmental attributes which combine to sustain life. While emphasis on food production and distribution must not be diminished, the population-food equation will never be stabilized by giving attention solely to the one variable — food. Nor will progress accrue unless regulation of man's own abundance takes place. In effect reduced hunger demands much more, and demonstrable changes are only achieved through related improvements in food, public health, water supply, education, housing, and so on. The only way to improve conditions is to become truly economical in the use of such basic resources as soil, water, and minerals, and at the same time to heed the fundamental laws of living nature and the obvious limitations of the globe.

On the whole, food and people can only be brought into reasonable balance through coordinated efforts (Fig. 9). A strategy, long overdue, needs to be formulated. Several action spheres need to be harnessed together, but primarily the following six: (1) food production, (2) population control, (3) better storage and utilization (both for food and feed), (4) nutritional requirements, (5) disease control, and (6) resource appraisal (soil, water, energy). Each measure taken needs to be coordinated or related to all the others, something which only has been done on rare occasions. There is considerable reason to maintain that sight of the overall goal — food for all — was lost in the struggle to achieve more immediate advantages.

Within the limited sphere of food production, top priority must be given to channeling the huge amounts of protein (half the ocean catches, one-fourth of the milk protein, and two-thirds of the oilseed protein) into human consumption. Second in line is a restructuring of the urbanization process to incorporate a recycling of the large amounts of organic waste for food (such as fish, mussels, squab, quail, etc.) or feed (yeast, algae, etc.). This will gradually become a third important source of food, supplementing agriculture and fish yields. The current experimentation with non-conventional foods will attain its greatest rationale within this framework and thereby move from its present tactical sphere into meaningful strategic operations.

Selected References

Abrams, C. *Man's Struggle for Shelter in an Urbanizing World*. Cambridge, Mass., The M.I.T. Press, 1966, 307 pp.

Albertson, P. and Barnett, M. (eds.). *Environment and Society in Transition*. Annals of the New York Academy of Sciences, Vol. 184, June 7, 1971, 699 pp.

Boughey, A. S. *Man and the Environment — An Introduction to Human Ecology and Evolution*. New York, The Macmillan Company, 1971, 472 pp.

Borgstrom, G. *Focal Points — The Seventies, Mankind's Decade of Destiny*. New York: The Macmillan Company, 1973, 322 pp.

Borgstrom, G. *Harvesting the Earth*. New York, Abelard-Schuman, 1973, 240 pp.

Borgstrom, G. *The Hungry Planet. The Modern World at the Edge of Famine*. New York, The Macmillan Company (1965), 1972, 2nd rev. ed., 552 pp. In paperback (1967), 1972, New York, Collier Books, 552 pp.

Borgstrom, G. *Too Many. A Study of Earth's Biological Limitations*. New York, The Macmillan Company, 1969, 368 pp. 2nd rev. ed. with subtitle *An Ecological Overview of Earth's Limitations*. New York, Collier Books, 1971, 400 pp.

Calder, N. *Eden Was No Garden: An Inquiry into the Environment of Man*. New York, Holt, Rinehart and Winston, 1967, 240 pp.

Canton, L. M. *A World Geography of Irrigation*. Edinburgh and London, Oliver and Boyd, 1967, 252 pp.

Davies, W. and Skidmore, C. L. (eds.). *Tropical Pastures*. London, Faber and Faber, 1966, 215 pp.

Duckham, A. N. and Masefield, G. B. *Farming Systems of the World*. London, Chatto & Windus, 1971, 542 pp.

Ehrlich, P. R. and Ehrlich, A. H. *Population Resources Environment. Issues in Human Ecology*. San Francisco, W. H. Freeman and Company, 1972 (1970), 509 pp.

Ehrlich, P. R., Ehrlich A. H., and Holdren, J. P. *Human Ecology — Problems and Solutions*. San Francisco: W. H. Freeman, 1973, 304 pp.

Fava, S. F. (ed.). *Urbanism in World Perspective: A Reader*. New York, Thomas Y. Crowell Company, 1968, 620 pp.

Fischer, J. *What You Can Do About Pollution Now*. Don Mills, Ontario, Longman Canada Ltd., 1971, 404 pp.

Forrester, J. W. *World Dynamics*. Cambridge, Mass., Wright-Allen Press, Inc., 1971, 142 pp.

Frankel, F. R. *India's Green Revolution. Economic Gains and Political Costs*. Princeton, N. J., Princeton University Press, 1971, 232 pp.

Fraser, D. *The People Problem. What You Should Know about Growing Population and Vanishing Resources*. Bloomington, Indiana University Press, 1971, 248 pp.

Glass, D. V. and Eversley, D. E. C. (eds.). *Population in History: Essays in Historical Demography*. London, Edward Arnold, Ltd., 1965, 692 pp.

Gulland, J. A. (ed.). *The Fish Resources of the Ocean*. West Byfleet, Surrey, England, Fishing News (Books), Ltd., 1971, 255 pp.

Higbee, E. *The Squeeze: Cities Without Space*. London, William Morrow & Company, 1960, 348 pp.

Holdren, J. and Herrera, P. *Energy — A Crisis in Power*. San Francisco and New York, Sierra Club, 1971, 252 pp.

International Conference on Family Planning Programs, *Family Planning and Population Programs: A Review of World Developments*. Proceedings of conference held in Geneva, August, 1965. Chicago and London, The University of Chicago Press, 1966, 848 pp.

Jacobs, J. *The Economy of Cities*. New York, Random House, 1969, 268 pp.

Janick, J. et al. (eds.). *Plant Agriculture. Readings from Scientific American*. San Francisco, W. H. Freeman and Company, 1970, 246 pp.

Jessop, N. M. *Biosphere — A Study of Life*. Englewood Cliffs, N. J., Prentice-Hall, Inc., 1970, 954 pp.

Johnson, S. *The Green Revolution*. New York, Harper Torchbooks, Harper & Row, 1972, 218 pp.

Meek, R.L. (ed.). *Marx and Engels on the Population Bomb*. Berkeley, Calif., Ramparts Press Inc., 1971, 215 pp.

Mühlenberg, F. *Wanderarbeit in Sudafrika*. Stuttgart, G. Fischer, 1967, 267 pp.

Mumford, L. *The Culture of Cities*. New York, Harcourt Brace Jovanovich, Inc., 1970 (1938), 586 pp.

Nicol, H. *The Limits of Man: An enquiry into the scientific bases of human population*. London, Constable, 1967, 283 pp.

Odum, H.T. *Environment, Power, and Society*. New York, Wiley-Interscience, 1971, 331 pp.

Petersen, W. *Population*. New York, The Macmillan Company, 2nd ed. 1969, 735 pp.

Reissman, L. *The Urban Process: Cities in Industrial Societies*. New York, The Free Press, 1970 (1964), 255 pp.

Rölvaag, O. E. *Giants in the Earth*. New York, Harper & Row, Perennial Library, 1965, 453 pp.

Russell-Hunter, W. D. *Aquatic Productivity: an introduction to some basic aspects of biological oceanography and limnology*. New York, The Macmillan Company, 1970, 306 pp.

San Pietro, A., Greer, F. A. and Army, T. J. (eds.). *Harvesting the Sun: Photosynthesis in Plant Life*. New York and London, 1967, 342 pp.

Scientific American *Energy and Power*. San Francisco, W.H. Freeman and Company, 1971, 144 pp.

Scott, F. D. (ed.). *World Migration in Modern Times*. Englewood Cliffs, N. J., Prentice-Hall, Inc., 1968, 177 pp.

Stewart, G. R. *Not So Rich As You Think*. Boston, Houghton Mifflin Company, 1967, 248 pp.

Thoman, R. S. and Conkling, E. C. *Geography of International Trade*. Englewood Cliffs, N. J., Prentice-Hall, Inc., 1967, 190 pp.

Thomlinson, R. *Population Dynamics: Causes and Consequences of World Demographic Change*. New York, Random House, 1965, 576 pp.

Toynbee, A. J. *Change and Habit — The Challenge of Our Time*. New York and

London, Oxford University Press, 1966, 240 pp.

Ward, B. and Dubos, R. *Only One Earth: The Care and Maintenance of a Small Planet.* Harmondsworth, Middlesex, England, Penguin Books, Ltd., 1972, 304 pp.

Ward, B., Runnalls, J. D., and D'Anjou, L. (eds.). *The Widening Gap.* New York and London, Columbia University Press, 1971, 372 pp.

Wharton, C. R. Jr. (ed.). *Subsistence Agriculture and Economic Development.* Chicago, Aldine Publishing Company, 1969, 481 pp.

Wrigley, E. A. *Population and History.* New York and Toronto, World University Library, McGraw-Hill Book Company, 1969, 256 pp.

Young, L. B. (ed.). *Population in Perspective.* New York, London, and Toronto, Oxford University Press, 1968, 460 pp.

Appendix:
Supplementary Tables

Conversion Table

One meter (m) = 3.28 feet

One kilometer (km) = 1,000 m =
0.62 mile

One square km (km²) = 0.386
sq. mile

One liter (ltr) = 0.264 gallon

One kilogram (kg) = 1,000 grams
(g) = 2.205 lbs

One metric ton = 2,205 lbs

One hectare (ha) = 100 ares =
2.471 acres

One are = 0.025 acre

One foot = 0.305 m

One mile = 1.61 km

One square mile = 2.59 km²

One gallon (4 qts) = 3.785 ltr

One pound (lb) = 0.4536 kg =
453.6 g

One acre = 0.405 ha = 40.5 ares

Table 1: World Population, by Continents, 1650-1950 (in millions)

Year	World Total	Africa	North America	Latin America	Asia	Europe*	Oceania	In Areas of European Settlement
1650	545	100	1	12	330	100	2	118
1750	730	95	2	12	479	140	2	158
1800	906	90	6	19	602	187	2	219
1850	1,171	95	26	33	749	266	2	355
1900	1,608	120	81	63	937	401	6	573
1930	2,070	164	134	108	1,120	534	10	784
1950	2,517	222	166	163	1,384	572	13	935

Source: A. M. Carr-Sanders, *World Population*, The Clarendon Press, Oxford, 1936, p. 42. UN Demographic Yearbook.
* including U.S.S.R.

Table 2: World Population, by Continents, 1950-1985 (in millions)

Year	Asia	Europe	U.S.S.R.	North America	Latin America	Africa	Oceania	Total
1950	1,384	392	180	166	163	222	13	2,517
1960	1,659	425	214	199	214	278	16	3,005
1970	2,056	462	243	227	283	344	19.5	3,635
1985	2,874	515	287	280	435	530	27	4,948
Estimated Increase								
1970-85	818	53	44	53	152	186	7.5	1,314

Source: U.N. Demographic Yearbook.

Table 3: World Population Percentage Distribution, 1650-1970 (A)

Continent/Year	1650	1750	1800	1850	1900	1930	1950	1960	1970
Asia	60.5	65.8	66.4	63.7	58.3	54.2	55.2	55.3	56.5
Europe	15.7	16.9	16.1	17.0	18.0	17.1	15.6	14.1	12.7
U.S.S.R. (Russia)	2.5	3.4	4.5	5.7	6.9	8.6	7.2	7.1	6.7
North America	0.18	0.27	0.66	2.2	5.0	6.5	6.6	6.6	6.3
Latin America	2.2	1.7	2.1	2.8	3.9	5.2	6.5	7.1	7.8
Oceania	0.36	0.27	0.22	0.17	0.37	0.48	0.51	0.53	0.54
Subtotal*	21.0	22.6	24.8	27.9	34.2	37.9	35.4	36.4	34.0
Africa	18.5	11.6	8.8	8.9	7.5	7.9	8.4	9.3	9.5

— The Western Climax —

* Europe plus areas receiving European emigrants.

Table 4: U.S. Immigration, 1951-1970 (in thousands)

From	1951-60	1961-70	From	1951-60	1961-70
Europe	2,515	1,252	South America	72.2	228.2
- Britain	195.6	230.5	- Colombia	17.6	70.3
- Italy	185.5	207	Caribbean	122.7	520.4
- Germany	477.8	200	- Cuba	78.3	256.8
- Greece	47.6	90			
Asia	147.5	430.9	Central America	44.6	97.7
- Philippines	18.1	101.6			
- China*	32.7	96.8	Africa	16.6	39.2

*chiefly from Taiwan

Table 5: U.S. Immigration, 1820-1950 (in millions)

1820-1850	0.25	1951-1960	2.52
1851-1900	16.67	1961-1970	3.32
1901-1950	20.20		

Chief Origin

Total	42.96		
Europe	34.57		3.56
- Germany	6.78	Latin America	2.19
- Italy	4.96	- Mexico	1.14
- Ireland	4.68	- Caribbean	0.62
- Britain	4.50	Asia	1.11
- Hungary*	4.28	Others	1.12
- USSR	3.34		
- Sweden	1.25		

* also Austria in early stage
** including Newfoundland
Source: Spec. Rept. Immigration & Naturalization Service.

Table 6: Canada — Immigration, 1852-1967 (in millions)

1852-1893	1.74	1933-1952	0.13
1894-1912	2.55	1943-1952	0.80
1913-1922	1.16	1953-1962	1.36
1923-1932	1.12	1963-1967	0.77

Table 7:   Asia, Population by Countries, 1951-1971 (in millions)

	1951	1956	1961	1966	1971
China	567	610	660	750	820
India	360	394	439	494	570
Pakistan	77	85	95	121	142
Indonesia	78	86	96	107	125
Japan	84	90	94	99	105
Philippines	21	24	28	34	39
Thailand	20	23	27	32	37
South Korea	20	22	25	29	33
Iran	17	19	21	24	29
Burma	19	21	23	25	28
North Vietnam	—	14	17	20	22
South Vietnam	9.8	12	14.5	17	18
Afghanistan	12	13	14.5	16	17
North Korea	—	9.4	11	12.5	14
Taiwan	7.7	9.2	11	13	14
Ceylon	7.9	8.9	10	11.5	13
Nepal	8.1	8.7	9.4	10.3	11.5
Malaysia	6.2	7.2	8.4	9.7	11.1
Cambodia	4.2	4.9	5.6	6.5	7.3
Hong Kong	2.0	2.6	3.2	3.7	4.3
Laos	1.4	1.6	1.9	2.0	3.1
Singapore	1.1	1.4	1.7	1.9	2.2
Mongolia	0.73	0.85	0.97	1.1	1.3
Ryukyu Islands	0.72	0.81	0.89	0.93	1.0
Bhutan	—	—	—	0.8	0.9
Sikkim	0.14	0.14	0.16	0.18	0.20
Sum	1,343	1,469	1,608	1,832	2,069
World Total	2,600	2,800	3,040	3,330	3,706
Asia Per Cent	51.7	52.4	52.9	55.0	55.7

Table 8: Arithmetic Densities of Population in 1971

A. *Immigration countries*

	Million sq. miles	Population millions	Number per sq. mile (A)
Argentina	1.073	24.7	21.9
Brazil	3.29	95.7	29.0
- Amazon Basin	2.32	5.7	4.1
- Remainder	0.97	90.0	91
Canada	3.61	21.8	6.0
Australia	2.98	12.8	4.3
New Zealand	0.044	2.9	65.0
South Africa	0.47	20.6	43.7
U.S.A.	3.55	207	58.3
U.S.S.R.	8.35	245	29.4

B. *Densely populated countries*

	Million sq. miles	Population millions	Number per sq. mile (A)
Japan	0.142	104.7	740
South & North Korea	0.085	47.2	555
China	2.90	820	283
India	1.26	570	453
Indonesia	0.74	124.9	169
- Java	0.049	83	1,690
Philippines	0.116	39.4	340
Thailand	0.198	37.4	189
Netherlands	0.013	13.1	975
Belgium	0.012	9.7	830
United Kingdom	0.089	56.3	630
West Germany	0.096	58.9	623
Italy	0.116	54.1	467

Table 9: Food Production Per Capita by Continents

	1948/52	1952/56	1961/65	1969/70
Satisfied World	92	100	115	126
Western Europe	87	100	119	125
U.S.S.R. & Eastern Europe	87	100	114	134
North America	99	100	113	118
Oceania	102	100	114	121
Hungry World	94	100	114	115
Latin America	97	100	114	117
Near East	90	100	113	115
Far East*	94	100	113	117
Africa	93	100	114	111

* excl. Cnina

Table 10:   Countries with Population of 20 Million or More in 1972

Rank		Approximate Mid-year Population (in millions)	Annual Percentage Growth	Number of Years to Double Population
1	China	786	1.7	41
2	India	585	2.5	28
3	U.S.S.R.	248	0.9	77
4	United States	209	1.0	70
5	Indonesia	129	2.9	24
6	Japan	106	1.2	58
7	Brazil	98	2.8	25
8	Bangladesh	80	3.3	21
9	Pakistan	67	3.3	21
10	West Germany	59	0.2	347
11	Nigeria	58	2.6	27
12	United Kingdom	57	0.5	139
13	Italy	55	0.7	99
14	Mexico	54	3.3	21
15	France	52	0.7	99
16	Philippines	41	3.3	21
17	Turkey	38	2.5	28
18	Thailand	39	3.3	21
19	UAR (Egypt)	36	2.8	25
20	Spain	34	1.0	70
21	Poland	34	0.9	77
22	South Korea	34	2.0	35
23	Iran	30	2.8	25
24	Burma	29	2.3	30
25	Ethiopia	26	2.1	33
26	Argentina	25	1.5	47
27	Colombia	23	3.4	21
28	Canada	22	1.7	41
29	North Vietnam	22	2.1	33
30	Romania	21	1.2	58
31	South Africa	21	2.4	29
32	Yugoslavia	21	0.9	77

Source: "1972 World Population Data Sheet," Population Reference Bureau, Inc.

Table 11: Gains in Cereal Production and Population by Continents, 1948-70 (in million metric tons)

	1948-52	1969-70	Gain (A)	Percent Increase (A)
Asia	268.3	476.8	208.5	75
million people	1,365	2,105	740	54
China	113.5	198.2	84.7	75
million people	547	840	293	53.5
U.S.S.R.	76.2	166.8	90.6	120
million people	184	241	57	31
Europe	112.4	186.5	74.0	66
million people	391	460	69	18
North America	162.8	227.6	64.8	40
million people	166	226	60	37
Africa	33.9	59.4	25.5	75
million people	220	352	132	60
Latin America	31.3	67.4	36.1	115
million people	162	280	118	73
Oceania	6.8	14.6	7.8	115
million people	12.4	19.1	6.7	54

Table 12: The Chinese Giant*, Ranking in Food Production
in per cent of world total. Annual averages, 1968-71.

A. Crops	I		II		III		IV	
Rice	China	33.3	India	20.7	Pakistan	7.0	Japan	6.1
Sweet Potato	China	64.5	Nigeria	9.2	Japan	2.3	Indonesia	1.5
Dry peas	U.S.S.R.	46.7	China	31.4	India	8.0	Europe	6.1
Soybeans	U.S.A.	68.8	China	24.4	Brazil	2.4	U.S.S.R.	1.2
Rapeseed	India	25.0	China	17.3	Canada	16.4	Poland	8.7
Peanuts	India	31.6	China	14.2	U.S.A.	7.3	Nigeria	7.2
Cottonseed	U.S.S.R.	19.2	U.S.A.	18.4	China	14.3	Pakistan	5.1
Dry beans	Brazil	20.2	India	18.8	China	12.2	Mexico	10.9
Wheat	U.S.S.R.	29.0	U.S.A.	12.4	China	9.5	India	6.2
B. Animal products								
Pork	China	25.1	U.S.A.	17.1	W. Germany	10.2	U.S.S.R.	9.8
Poultry meat	U.S.A.	40.7	China	18.5	U.S.S.R.	5.8	France	4.0
Eggs	U.S.A.	20.1	China	16.2	U.S.S.R.	10.5	Japan	7.9
Mutton	Australia	11.8	U.S.S.R.	11.3	China	8.8	New Zealand	8.2
Beef	U.S.A.	25.8	U.S.S.R.	12.0	Argentina	6.5	China	5.6

* China's population constitutes 23.4% of the world's peoples.

Table 13: Yield Comparisons in Selected Countries, 1969-70
(in 100 kilograms per hectare) (A)

Wheat		*Rice*		*Sorghum*	
Netherlands	44.1	Spain	62.9	U.A.R. (Egypt)	39.8
East Germany	35.2	Japan	56.0	Bulgaria	32.6
Mexico	27.6	U.A.R. (Egypt)	52.7	Mexico	24.8
U.A.R. (Egypt)	26.0	U.S.A.	49.6	U.S.A.	18.3
U.S.A.	20.7	China	27.6		
U.S.S.R.	13.1	Indonesia	20.0		
Argentina	13.0	Thailand	18.6		
		India	16.5		

Lentils		*Castor beans*		*Beans (dry)*	
U.A.R. (Egypt)	14.5	Peru	17.9	U.S.S.R.	16.7
U.S.A.	12.7	Paraguay	13.0	U.A.R. (Egypt)	15.0
		U.S.A.	9.5	Poland	14.6
				U.S.A.	14.0

Peanuts		*Sugar Cane*		*Cow Peas*	
Turkey	24.6	Peru	1,487	Iraq	8.4
U.S.A.	21.2	Ethiopia	1,440	U.S.A.	6.1
Nigeria	11.4	U.S.A.	970		

Sesame Seed		*Soybeans*		*Sunflower Seed*	
Guatemala	10.0	Mexico	20.6	Kenya	30.2
Saudi Arabia	9.5	U.S.A.	18.3	U.S.S.R.	13.1
Syria	8.9			U.S.A.	9.8
U.S.A.	5.3				
India	1.9				

Table 14: Global Animal Production
Distribution in per cent of world total.
Annual averages, 1969-71. (A)

	Milk*	Meat**	Eggs
Europe	37.8	26.7	27.9
North America	15.4	22.5	21.4
U.S.S.R.	20.7	10.9	10.9
Australia & New Zealand	3.4	3.8	1.1
Japan	1.2	1.1	8.3
SW (28% of world population)	78.5	65.0	69.6
China	0.8	14.0†	15.7

*   India and Pakistan, 9.7 (half of which is buffalo milk)
** excluding horses and poultry
†   Mostly pork

Table 15: Fish in Animal Protein Intake (A)
Annual averages, 1967-68.

HW	Per cent	SW	Per cent
Cambodia	83.5	Japan	52.5
Indonesia	67.5	Portugal	38
Ceylon	62	Iceland	30.5
Ghana	59	Norway	19
Philippines	50	Denmark	18
Thailand	50	Spain	17
South Korea	49.5	Sweden	14
Senegal	46	Chile	13
Malaysia	45	East Germany	13
Ivory Coast	43.5	Italy	8.6
Jamaica	41.5	U.S.S.R.	8.4
Nigeria	38	United Kingdom	7.5
Venezuela	28	Poland	7.0
China	18	Australia	5.1
India	11	Canada	4.8
Mexico	5.6	U.S.A.	4.7
		New Zealand	4.4
		Argentina	2.6

Table 16: Tilled Land by Continents, 1969

	Million hectares	*Per Cent (A)*		*Ares per capita (A)*
WORLD	1,424			39.0
World Ranking				
1. Asia	449	31.5	*Sum*	21.2
- India	164	11.5	—	30.3
- China	110	7.5	—	13.2
2. U.S.S.R.	233	16.5	48	96.7
3. North America	220	15.5	63.5	98.1
4. Africa	204	14.5	78	60.5
5. Europe	148	10.5	98.5	32.4
6. Latin America	123	8.5	97.0	44.7
- South America	90	6.5	—	48.3
7. Oceania	47	3.0	100.0	248.0

Table 17: Irrigated Land, end of 1960's
(in millions of hectares)

China	76.0	Asia		
India	27.5	(excluding China, India,		
U.S.A.	15.0	Pakistan)		16.1
U.S.S.R.	12.5	- Indonesia	5.6	
Pakistan	12.0	- Japan	3.2	
Middle East	14.0	- Korea	1.0	
- Iran	4.7	- Thailand	1.9	
- Iraq	3.7	- Vietnam	1.5	
- Egypt	2.8	= Philippines	1.0	
- Turkey	1.6	Europe		5.7
Latin America	9.3	- Spain	2.5	
– Mexico	4.3	- Italy	2.4	

Table 18:   Ranking in Fertilizer (NPK)*
Consumption 1969-70 (A)

Top Group

	kg/hectare arable land		kg per capita
Netherlands	690.0	New Zealand	161.7
Belgium	590.0	Ireland	130.8
Japan	406.3	Denmark	118.9
W. Germany	374.5	Finland	98.8
E. Germany	311.6	E. Germany	93.7
Cuba	234.1	Australia	89.2

	kg/hectare	kg per capita
U.S.A.	82.6	33.5
U.S.S.R.	34.5	13.2

Bottom Group

	kg/hectare		kg per capita
India	8.52	Indonesia	1.92
Pakistan	13.9	India	2.60
Indonesia	17.6	China	3.90
Brazil	20.2	Brazil	6.62
Mexico	22.4	Mexico	10.9
China	29.4	Japan	22.3

* N = Nitrogen, P = Phosphate, K = Potassium

Table 19: Man's Dominion in Selected Countries, 1969-70
(in million PE units)

	Humans	Livestock (A)	Total (A)	Ratio of Livestock to Humans (A)
Japan	102.32	79.48	181.80	0.78
Indonesia	116.98	115.07	232.05	0.98
U.A.R. (Egypt)	32.47	49.37	81.84	1.52
Trinidad and Tobago	1.04	1.72	2.76	1.65
Jamaica	1.96	3.39	5.35	1.73
China	832.10	1,763.26	2,595.36	2.12
India	536.98	1,486.33	2,023.31	2.77
Pakistan	127.50	379.19	506.69	2.97
Italy	53.17	159.21	212.38	2.99
Spain	32.95	99.75	132.70	3.03
United Kingdom	55.53	184.19	239.12	3.32
WORLD	3,647.08	14,456.80	10,103.88	3.96
U.S.S.R.	240.33	1,319.04	1,559.37	5.50
U.S.A.	203.22	1,255.55	1,458.77	6.18
Mexico	48.93	326.50	374.43	6.67
Brazil	90.84	1,208.05	1,298.89	13.30
Argentina	23.98	495.58	519.56	20.67
Australia	12.30	356.44	368.74	29.00
Uruguay	2.78	92.64	95.49	32.51
New Zealand	2.78	135.32	138.10	48.68

Table 20:   The Hunger Gap: Per capita intake of calories
and proteins (in grams per day), 1966-68

HW	Calories	Plant protein	Animal protein (excl. Fish)	Fish protein	Total protein
Monsoon Asia excluding Japan	2,080	43.8	3.0	5.2	52.0
- China	2,050	49.3	6.5	1.4	57.2
- India	1,940	42.3	5.0	0.6	47.9
Near & Middle East	2,310	57.8	10.8	1.2	69.8
Africa	2,170	47.6	6.9	4.0	58.5
Latin America (excluding Argentina & Uruguay)	2,350	43.5	20.0	4.1	67.6
Average	2,100	47.9	5.4	4.3	57.6
SW					
Europe	3,060	43.8	39.2	4.2	87.2
U.S.S.R.	3,180	56.4	32.8	3.0	92.2
North America	3,250	29.3	63.8	3.2	96.3
Oceania	3,300	36.2	67.0	3.2	106.4
Argentina & Uruguay	3,120	42.0	60.7	1.0	103.7
Japan	2,450	45.4	15.5	14.2	75.1
Israel	2,930	46.6	40.4	2.7	89.7
South Africa	2,730	48.7	24.7	3.8	77.2
Average	3,070	40.8	44.6	3.7	89.1

Table 21: Consumption of Basic Foods in the late 1960's.
(in kilograms per person per year)

SW	Sugar	Visible fat	Meat	Milk	Tubers	Beans Nuts
Australia	58	14	111	237	53	4.4
U.S.A.	51	24	112	246	46	8.5
Netherlands	49	27	58	248	92	5.2
Sweden	41	20	52	264	88	2.6
United Kingdom	48	23	76	218	104	6.7
France	36	26	94	233	100	5.2
Italy	27	21	48	126	47	9.6
Spain	26	18	44	152	112	11.8
Greece	21	19	41	166	59	17.0
Japan	24	9	15	48	59	17.4
HW						
Brazil	38	5.5	34	75	185	32.2
Peru	29	8	23	63	207	11.0
Mexico	40	8.8	20	57	13	28.3
Turkey	15	11.0	14.4	81	40	13.0
U.A.R. (Egypt)	20	5.5	13	44	12	11.8
Kenya	12	1.9	20	37	114	26.1
India	16	3.3	1.5	42	34	18.0
China	4	2.6	17	3.3	91	34.4
Pakistan	19	5.3	4.0	77	16	5.9
Indonesia	6	3.5	4.1	1.1	119	12.6

Table 22:   Trade Acreage Balance by Continents, 1965-67 (A)
(in million hectares)

	Import	Export	Net
EUROPE	63.6	5.9	47.7
- Western, incl. Southern	53.2	11.1	42.1
- Eastern	10.4	4.8	5.6
ASIA	52.3	26.2	26.1
- Japan	11.0	0.1	10.9
- India	13.5	7.5	6.0
- China	7.3	3.0	4.3
- Hong Kong	2.6	0.1	2.5
U.S.S.R.	7.7	2.3	5.5
LATIN AMERICA	21.0	32.1	-11.1
- South America	11.6	26.6	-15.0
- Argentina	0.05	18.4	-18.4
- Central America	2.0	3.2	-1.2
- Mexico	0.80	1.78	-0.98
- Caribbean	7.4	2.3	5.1
AFRICA	10.9	24.3	-13.6
-Nigeria	0.2	2.4	-2.2
-Ghana	0.5	1.9	-1.4
OCEANIA	2.2	15.8	-13.6
- Australia	0.4	12.7	-12.3
- New Zealand	0.12	3.99	-3.4
NORTH AMERICA	8.1	49.7	-41.6
- U.S.A.	6.6	37.8	-31.2
- Canada	1.5	11.8	-10.3

Table 23:   Net Import of Beef, 1969-70
(in 1,000 metric tons)

World Ranking		Kg/ capita (A)	World Ranking		Kg/ capita (A)
1.	U.S.A.	490.6	2.4	5. Spain	81.0	2.4
2.	U.K.	295.8	5.3	6. Greece	61.2	6.9
3.	Italy	275.8	5.1	7. Israel	36.5	12.6
4.	W. Germany	138.8	2.3	8. Switzerland	32.9	5.2

Table 24: United Kingdom and India: Grain Importation, 1960-69
(in million metric tons)

	U. K.	India
1960	9.23	5.15
1961	9.05	3.61
1962	10.39	3.58
1963	8.78	4.62
1964	8.47	6.39
1965	8.96	7.59
1966	8.46	10.19
1967	8.39	9.06
1968	8.30	5.66
1969	8.98	3.98
Total	89.01	59.83
Population million (1969)	55.3	526
Per capita (kilograms)	1.61	0.11
Ratio	14.62	

Per capita: U.K. imported almost 15 times more than India.

Table 25: Production - Trade, Global Balance, 1969-70
(in million metric tons)

	Production	Trade	Trade as a Percentage of Production (A)	
Wheat	313.5	50.9	16.1	
Rice	301.1	10.1	3.4	
Corn	265.9	27.9	10.4	
Barley	132.7	6.8	5.1	
Soybeans	45.8	9.1	19.8	
- cake & meal*	—	4.8	10.5	30.3
Groundnuts	17.4	1.42	8.2	
- cake & meal*	—	1.60	9.3	17.5
Potato	294.5	3.48	1.2	
Onion	10.9	1.04	9.5	
Meat**	78.6	6.0	7.7	
Milk	398.1	23.5	6.2	
Eggs	20.2	0.53	2.6	
Fish	64	34†	53	

* bean and nut equivalent
** excluding horses and poultry
† Live weight equivalent, 27.6 constitutes fishmeal, some from stored lots and from viscera.

Table 26:   Wheat Importation, 1968-69

	million metric tons	Kg/ per capita (A)
Cuba	1.17	142.8
Israel	0.367	135.3
Lebanon	0.280	110.1
Libya	0.202	107.9
Netherlands	1.33	104.3
Martinique	0.032	94.5
Trinidad	0.097	94.3
Czechoslovakia	1.31	91.2
Norway	0.327	85.3
Britain	4.53	81.7
Guadeloupe	0.026	79.9
Belgium	0.810	76.6
East Germany	1.19	69.9
Venezuela	0.030	69.9
Mauritius	0.057	69.2
Switzerland	0.391	63.2
U.A.R. (Egypt)	1.90	59.2
Algeria	0.562	42.8
West Germany	2.15	35.5
Poland	1.13	34.8
Portugal	0.294	30.9
Italy	1.40	26.4

Table 27:   Europe: Protein Balance (A)
(in million metric tons)

Production 1969-70		Import 1968-69		Per cent of world trade
Milk	4.81	Cereals	2.56	45
Meat	3.81	Oilseed cake & meal	2.42	93
Eggs	0.33	Soybeans	1.95	58.5
	8.95	Peanuts	0.30	85
		Misc.	0.26	76
		Fish meal (oceans)	1.69	70
		Total	9.18	

Table 28: U.S. Soybean Export (in million bushels)

Importers	1967-68	Per Cent	1969-70	Per Cent
West Europe	150.1	54.2	226.7	52.7
Japan	71.8	25.9	102.1	23.7
Canada*	29.3	10.6	53.9	12.7
Total	276.8	90.7	430.7	89.1

* including transshipments to Japan and Europe

World Ranking	1967-68	Per Cent	1969-70	Per Cent
1. Japan	71.8	25.9	102.1	23.7
2. Netherlands	39.8	14.4	57.4	13.3
3. Canada	29.3	10.6	53.9	12.7
4. West Germany	31.3	11.3	47.4	11.0
5. Spain	30.3	10.9	37.5	8.9
6. Italy	15.6	5.6	25.7	6.0
7. Taiwan	13.6	4.9	20.4	4.7
8. Denmark	13.7	4.9	19.9	4.6
9. Belgium	9.5	3.4	14.7	3.4
10. Israel	8.0	2.9	10.7	2.5
11. France	0.5	0.8	9.1	2.1

Table 29: Soybean Importation, 1969
(in 1,000 metric tons)

World Ranking in Kg/capita	Thousand metric tons	Population million	Kg/capita (A)	Protein Kg/capita (A)
1. Denmark	416.1	4.9	85.0	28.2
2. Israel	207.9	2.8	74.0	25.8
3. Netherlands	915.1	12.9	71.0	24.8
4. Norway	177.3	3.8	46.7	16.7
5. Taiwan	472.2	13.5	35.0	12.2
6. Spain	1,026.5	32.7	31.4	10.9
7. Belgium	256.2	9.7	26.4	9.2
8. Japan	2,590.6	102.1	25.4	8.9
9. West Germany	1,397.8	58.1	24.0	8.4
10. Canada	384.3	21.1	18.3	6.4
11. Italy	606.7	53.1	11.4	3.9
12. United Kingdom	324.4	55.7	5.9	2.1

Table 30: World Trade Peanut Cake and Meal, 1967-69
(in million metric tons)

Exporters		Importers	
World	1.44	World	1.29
India	0.60	United Kingdom	0.35
Senegal	0.22	France	0.18
Nigeria	0.16	West Germany	0.15
Brazil	0.13	Czechoslovakia*	0.15
Argentina	0.09	Hungary	0.10
Sudan	0.04	Denmark	0.07
		Japan	0.07
Subtotal	1.24	Sweden	0.05
		Subtotal	1.12

* 1967-68

Table 31: Banana Trade 1968-69
(in million metric tons)

Import Total	5.29			Export Total	5.63		
World Ranking		Per Cent		World Ranking		Per Cent	
1. U.S.A.	1.65	31.3	Sum	1. Ecuador	1.22	21.7	Sum
2. Japan	0.69	13.1	44.4	2. Honduras	0.88	15.6	37.3
3. West Germany	0.56	10.6	55.0	3. Costa Rica	0.63	11.2	48.5
4. France	0.44	8.3	63.3	4. Panama	0.57	10.1	50.6
5. Italy	0.33	6.2	69.5	5. Colombia	0.37	6.6	65.2
6. Canada	0.19	3.6	73.1	6. Taiwan	0.36	6.4	69.6

Table 32: Degree of Self-Sufficiency in Major Plant Commodities, 1967-69 (in million metric tons)

	Production	Net Import (A)	Consumption (A)	% Import (A)
Jamaica				
Wheat	—	0.157	0.157	100
Cereals	0.007	0.204	0.211	97
UK				
Wheat	3.58	4.34	7.92	54.6
Cereals	13.78	7.97	21.75	37.1
Netherlands				
Wheat	0.70	0.56	1.26	44.5
Cereals	1.71	2.90	4.61	63
Pulses	0.050	0.232	0.28	83
Switzerland				
Wheat	0.41	0.39	0.80	48.7
Cereals	0.66	1.23	1.89	65.2
Belgium				
Wheat	0.84	0.49	1.33	36.8
Cereals	1.83	2.44	4.27	57.3
Italy				
Wheat	9.61	0.76	10.37	7.3
Cereals	15.39	6.66	22.00	30
West Germany				
Wheat	6.00	1.17	7.17	16.3
Cereals	18.67	5.28	23.95	22
Denmark				
Wheat	0.95	0.03	0.48	6.2
Cereals	6.28	0.25	6.53	3.8
China				
Wheat	29.2	3.91	33.1	11.8
Cereals	195.4	3.26	198.7	1.6
India				
Wheat	19.3	4.78	24.1	19.8
Cereals	101.4	6.23	107.6	5.8
Indonesia				
Rice	16.5	0.56	17.1	3.3
Cereals	17.6	0.83	18.43	4.5

Table 33: The World's 25 Largest Cities, 1972 (in millions)

		Administrative unit	Metropolitan area
1.	Tokyo (Japan)	8.84	22.2
2.	New York City (U.S.)	7.90	17.5
3.	Shanghai (China)	7.80	10.7
4.	London (U.K.)	7.42	10.7
5.	Moscow (U.S.S.R.)	7.04	10.0
6.	Bombay (India)	5.97	6.75
7.	Sao Paulo (Brazil)	5.92	8.05
8.	Djakarta (Indonesia)	5.90	6.60
9.	Seoul (So. Korea)	5.54	5.90
10.	Cairo (U.A.R.)	4.96	6.60
11.	Peking (China)	4.75	7.80
12.	Rio de Janeiro (Brazil)	4.25	7.00
13.	Delhi (India)	3.69	4.48
14.	Leningrad (U.S.S.R.)	3.56	4.68
15.	Tientsin (China)	3.50	3.90
16.	Chicago (U.S.)	3.33	7.68
17.	Calcutta (India)	3.14	9.10
18.	Madrid (Spain)	3.12	3.53
19.	Mukden (China)	3.00	—
20.	Osaka (Japan)	2.98	13.4
21.	Buenos Aires (Argentina)	2.97	8.63
22.	Mexico City (Mexico)	2.90	9.00
23.	Teheran (Iran)	2.88	3.25
24.	Los Angeles (U.S.)	2.80	8.83
25.	Rome (Italy)	2.78	3.00

Table 34: The Global Energy Balance and the Energy Gap, 1968-69 (in billion coal equivalents - tons)

World Total   6.86

		Per Cent	
*SW**			
North America	2.38	34.7	*Sum*
Europe	2.07	30.0	64.7
U.S.S.R.	1.01	14.7	79.4
Japan	0.28	4.1	83.5
Oceania	0.073	1.1	84.6
*HW**			
China	0.450	6.2	
Asia (excluding Middle East,			*Sum*
China and Japan)	0.286	4.2	10.4
Latin America	0.229	3.3	13.7
Africa	0.101	1.6	15.3
Middle East	0.064	1.0	16.3

* SW (= the Satisfied World) holds 28% of the world's population, HW (= the Hungry World) 72%.

Table 35: Food in the National Energy Account, 1969 (A)
(in kilogram coal equivalents (CE) per capita)

SW	Food	National Energy Account	Per Cent
U.S.A.	635	10,774	5.9
East Germany	493	5,697	8.7
U.S.S.R.	388	4,199	9.2
Sweden	549	5,768	9.5
Japan	292	2,828	10.3
Poland	434	4,052	10.7
Australia	580	5,208	11.1
Denmark	598	5,142	14.5
Cuba	264	1,053	26
New Zealand	670	2,623	25
Taiwan	254	874	29

HW	Food	National Energy Account	Per Cent
Peru	252	623	41
Fiji	210	407	52
Guatemala	234	176	76
India	154	193	80
Ecuador	213	270	80
Reunion	250	268	93
U.A.R. (Egypt)	230	221	104
El Salvador	156	170	109
Indonesia	119	98	122
Mauritius	220	161	137
China	173	120	144

Table 36: Balance Between the United States and
India in Food, Energy, and Water, 1969 (A)

Per capita/day	U.S.	India	Ratio U.S./India
Food			
Calories	3,300	1,900	1.65
Primary calories	11,900	2,910	4.10
Total protein (grams)	98.6	49.4	2.00
Animal protein (grams)	71.5	5.6	12.75
Energy (kilograms)	10,774	193	55.80
Water (for food)*			
(tons per capita per day)	14.4	1.8	7.97

* in agricultural production

Table 37: Energy Comparisons: Food and Fertilizers, 1969
(in kilogram coal equivalents (CE) per capita)

	Food	Fertilizers	Relation of Fertilizers to Food (in percent)		Food	Fertilizers	Relation of Fertilizers to Food (in percent)
Fiji	180	575	319	Poland	434	375	87
U.A.R.	230	530	230	Indonesia	119	96	80
Peru	252	534	211	Ecuador	215	168	78
El Salvador	156	308	181	Australia	580	428	74
New Zealand	670	809	121	Reunion	250	186	74
China	173	195	113	Mauritius	220	133	61
Denmark	598	595	100	Sweden	549	297	54
East Germany	493	469	95	U.S.S.R.	388	162	42
Guatemala	234	220	94	Japan	292	112	38
Cuba	276	257	93	U.S.A.	635	210	33

Index

(Figures in italics indicate pages upon which illustrations occur.)